COMPLETELY REVISED AND EXPANDED

FAST FOOD FACTS

Complete Nutrition Information on More Than 1,500 Menu Items in 37 of the Largest Fast Food Chains

Marion J. Franz, M.S., R.D., C.D.E.

FOURTH EDITION

CHRONIMED
PUBLISHING

Minneapolis, Minnesota

Library of Congress Cataloging-in-Publication Data
Franz, Marion J.
Fast food facts. /Marion J. Franz-[Updated and revised.]
ISBN 1-56561-043-1
1. Convenience foods-Composition-Tables. 2. Food-Composition-Tables. 3. Diabetes-Nutritional aspects.
4. Fast food restaurants-United States.

Editor: Karol Carstensen
Cover & Text Design: MacLean & Tuminelly
Photography: Paul Lundquist

Printed in the United States of America

10 9 8 7 6 5 4 3 2 1

© 1983, revised 1987, 1990, 1994
International Diabetes Center

CHRONIMED Publishing
PO Box 47945
Minneapolis, MN 55447-9727

Exchange lists and nutritive values based on *Exchange Lists for Meal Planning* © 1986, American Diabetes Association and The American Dietetic Association.

Table of Contents

In Canada:

Eating Out in America

More than half the American population, over 133 million people, eat out or buy to-go foods in an average day. This is big business. In 1990, total food service sales topped $238.8 billion, up 458% from $42.8 billion 20 years earlier.

Dinner is the most popular meal eaten out. On a typical day, 23% of all adults patronize restaurants for dinner. Lunch is a close second, with 22% of all adults eating out. A smaller number eat breakfast (5%) and between-meal snacks (4%) out.

Today 4 out of 10 consumers claim to have improved their eating habits in restaurants. According to a National Restaurant Association Survey, consumers stated they were using less salt (23%), eating less fat (20%) and eating fewer fried foods. But we often say one thing and do another, and this is certainly true when dining out.

Restaurants are offering more low-fat fare but, according to industry reports, the demand for "all-you-can-eat" specials and for high-fat, high-sugar desserts is still appreciable. Customers still seem to yearn for yummy, juicy calories as quickly and cheaply as possible. Better choices may be available, but even people who eat out frequently may consider it a "treat," and be reluctant to take advantage of the healthier fare offered.

Fast-food is a distinctly American part of this food service business. The majority of customers, 82%, order fast-food at the counter and eat in the restaurant. However, 78% use drive-thru windows, and 76% purchase carryout. Other popular dining options include home delivery and carryout from supermarkets, convenience stores, delis and tableservice restaurants.

Eating out more often, and eating more fast food, may seem incompatible with America's ever-growing interest in nutrition and fitness. However, if you are one of the estimated 200 fast-food customers ordering one or more hamburgers every second, don't despair. You can eat fast food without sacrificing your health or your waistline.

The Problem With Fast Food

Fast foods provide ample protein and some vitamins and minerals, but they also tend to provide large amounts of saturated fats, cholesterol, and sodium—not to mention calories.

Calories

The greatest nutrition problem with most fast foods is the high number of calories. You can easily gulp down half the total number of calories your body needs each day, plus your entire sodium allotment, from a single fast-food meal. For example, if you have a fried fish sandwich, a milk shake, and large french fries, you've eaten 1100 calories, 45 grams of fat, and 1170 milligrams of sodium. This is over half the calories and sodium most adults need in a day.

Sample menus can range from an appropriate level of 400 to 500 calories to a grand total of 1400 to 1500 calories! A quarter-pound burger with cheese, large fries, and a shake contain about 1200 calories and 52 grams of fat. A 1200-calorie meal might be okay for an active teenage boy, but it provides about 50% of the daily calories needed to maintain the weight of a 165-pound man, and 70% of the calories needed by a 128-pound woman. In fact, for someone on a diet, 1200 calories is practically the whole day's allotment.

Where do all the calories in fast-food come from? Fat.

Fat

On the average, 40% to 60% of calories in fast foods come from fat. Rich sources of fast-food fat are cheese, mayonnaise, and the popular method of deep-frying.

Chicken and fish items are often thought of as the best choices at fast-food restaurants because they are traditionally lower in calories and fat than beef or other red meats. However, these choices are usually worse than beef because they are often coated with batter and deep-fried. The batter acts as a sponge, absorbing large amounts of fat during the frying process. Chicken and fish products may, in the end, contain more fat and calories than a hamburger or roast beef sandwich. You can usually order a roast beef sandwich AND fries for less fat than you get in a fried chicken breast sandwich alone!

Sodium

Some menu items also contain large amounts of sodium (salt), which can contribute to high blood pressure. The average American eats 10 to 60 times the sodium needed per day.

Several fast-food sandwiches contain 1500 to 2000 milligrams of sodium (2/3 to 3/4 teaspoon of salt), more than half the daily recommended maximum sodium intake of 3000 milligrams (1 to 1/2 teaspoons of salt). For instance, a single cheeseburger can contain 1400 milligrams of sodium and a fish dinner more than 1800 milligrams. Add salted french fries, onion rings, a milk shake, or excessive amounts of condiments like catsup, mustard, and pickles, and the sodium level of your meal skyrockets.

It's difficult to know by taste how much sodium is in food. Surprisingly, french fries can be the lowest. Salt is sprinkled on before and after frying, which makes fries taste salty, but much of the added salt stays on the paper container.

Sugar

Sugar is added to food to improve taste as well as appearance. The greatest sources of sugar are soft drinks and shakes. Shakes get most of their calories from sugar. A typical small (10-ounce) shake contains about 9 to 11 teaspoons of sugar, as much as a 12-ounce can of regular soda pop, plus 2 to 4 teaspoons of fat and 350 to 400 calories. A 14-ounce shake has 13-15 teaspoons of sugar (760 calories), and a 20-ounce shake has 19-21 teaspoons of sugar (990 calories).

Fiber

The average American consumes 10 to 20 grams of dietary fiber per day, about half the usual recommended intake. Eating fast foods could be one reason for this dismal statistic.

Fast foods, except for salads and coleslaw (recent additions to fast-food menus), are generally low in fiber. Fruits, vegetables, and whole grains, which are good sources of fiber, are not often offered by fast-food restaurants. A great way to add more fiber to your meal is by adding garbanzo beans, those small, round, tan legumes (also known as chickpeas), to your salad.

Fast-Food Tips

For most people, including those with diabetes, an occasional fast-food meal will not upset an otherwise well-balanced diet. What you order and how often you order it are the real issues. Like many other lifestyle concerns, moderation is important.

The following tips will help you make the right fast-food choices for you.

- **The key to overall nutrition survival is selection and serving size.** You need to be familiar with choices available on a fast-food menu. This book can help you make better food and beverage choices.

- **Look for meals that meet these guidelines:**

	Men	Women
Calories	800-900	500-600
Fat, grams per meal	30-35	20-25
Sodium, milligrams per meal	<1000	<1000

  If the totals for a meal exceed any of the above, be especially careful in your food choices the rest of the day.

- **Eat only at meal times.** The average calorie count of a fast-food meal is 685, which is not outrageously high. However, many people eat fast-food items as snacks rather than meals, adding a hefty average of 427 calories to their regular daily intake. That can easily put people well over their daily limits.

- **Buy small. Avoid menu choices labeled "jumbo," "giant," or "deluxe."** Larger serving sizes mean not only additional calories, but generally more fat, cholesterol and sodium. Caution is required.

- **If you have a fast food meal, try to balance it out with the rest of your day's food choices.** Add additional servings of fruits, vegetables, low-fat milk, and whole-grain foods to your other meals. Remember, not only is it important to make healthy selections, it's also important to eat three meals a day. It's tempting to skip breakfast and lunch when you are dieting to lose weight, or when life gets too hectic to think about eating. And, although exercise is important, don't skip lunch in order to find time to exercise. Both are important!

- **Limit salad dressings, mayonnaise, mayonnaise-based dressings, and other sauces.** Each tablespoon of dressing adds an extra 100 to 200 calories to a sandwich or salad.

- **Share.** Fries, a large sandwich, a baked potato, or dessert will taste even better when shared with a friend. Or take half home for another meal.

Making the Best Fast-Food Choice

Whether eating out or at home, all of us should try to eat a variety of foods in moderate portions, with no more than 30% of our daily calories coming from fat. Consider these suggestions.

Burgers—Order A Single and Skip the Fixings

Scaling down to single patties and selecting basic meat items results in a lower-fat sandwich. A regular hamburger (or even two plain burgers) has less fat than a double burger with cheese and special sauces. Cheese adds 100 calories per slice as well as added fat and sodium, and sauces add even more of the same. A McDonald's McLean burger is lower in fat, but a plain quarter pounder is not such a bad choice either. So if you've got a double-decker appetite, skip the usual dressings and pile on the lettuce and tomatoes instead.

Small burgers range from 180 to 350 calories, with about 10 grams of fat. A small burger may not satisfy your hunger, so fill up on salad with low-fat dressings or even a baked potato.

Compare:

Regular Hamburger, lettuce and tomatoes *with*	270 calories	12 gm fat	504 mg sodium
Large Cheeseburger with triple meat	800 calories	51 gm fat	1211 mg sodium

GOOD CHOICES:	Calories	Gm Fat	Mg Sodium
Hamburger	257	9	490
Small Fries	220	12	110
	477	21	600
or			
Quarter Pounder	410	20	645
Side Salad with	42	2	145
Lite Vinagrette Dressing	452	22	790

Chicken and Fish—Breading Traps the Fat

Chicken and fish are often perceived as light fare. They start out very healthful, but battering, breading, or deep-frying cancels out their normal, low-fat advantages. Deep-fried chicken items often have the highest calories on the menu. Deep-fried chicken sandwiches average 500 to 700 calories and contribute about 4 to 6 1/2 teaspoons of fat. A fish filet sandwich has 400 to 500 calories, including 4 teaspoons of fat.

The best choice is a grilled chicken breast. If fried is your only choice, choose regular coating over extra crispy varieties (which soak up more oil during cooking) and save as many as 86 calories per piece. Even better, peel off the skin and lose 100 calories plus most of the fat and excess sodium. By ordering separate pieces instead of combinations or whole dinners, you save calories as well. Order mashed potatoes and gravy instead of fries and save another 200 calories.

If possible, stick to baked fish. It has half the fat and calories of fried fish and is lower in sodium. Skip the tartar sauce (about 120 calories for 2 tablespoons) and use cocktail sauce (only 35 calories) or lemon juice (0 calories).

Compare:

Grilled Chicken Breast Fillet in Bun	340 calories	12 gm fat	565 mg sodim
with			
Deep-Fried Breaded Chicken Sandwich	688 calories	40 gm fat	957 mg sodium

GOOD CHOICES:	Calories	Gm Fat	Mg Sodium
Grilled Chicken Entree	206	5	420
Baked Potato with 2 Tbsp. Sour Cream	90	5	7
Green Beans	<u>13</u>	<u>tr</u>	<u>22</u>
	309	11	507
or			
Swordfish, 5 oz.	150	6	410
Rice Pilaf	140	3	390
Vegetable	<u>25</u>	<u>0</u>	<u>20</u>
	315	9	820

Sandwiches—Many Low-Fat Options

Regular and junior-sized roast beef, ham-and-cheese, and turkey sandwiches can be the best choices at fast-food restaurants. Consider the difference between a small roast beef sandwich (230 calories) and the deluxe version (552 calories). Skipping the mayonnaise topping (use mustard or horseradish instead) saves at least 100 calories per tablespoon.

For lunch, consider sandwiches made with whole-grain breads and lean meats like roast beef, French dip, turkey breast, or lean ham. But add bacon, cheese, and sauces, and you also add calories and fat.

Super hot dogs with cheese have more than 7 teaspoons of fat, 590 calories, and 1360 milligrams of sodium (more than 1/2 teaspoon of salt). Add a large malt with 1060 calories—about 25 teaspoons of sugar—and you're in trouble. Stick to a single hamburger with lettuce and tomato (or a roast beef sandwich), a regular frozen cone, and a diet soda—all for only 506 calories and 710 milligrams of sodium.

Croissant sandwiches are also high in calories and fat. Just the croissant averages 200 to 500 calories compared with 135 calories in a whole-grain or white bun. Croissant sandwiches average 400 to 600 calories. That is high compared with an average 350 calories for a plain roast beef sandwich, 340 calories for a chicken breast sandwich, or 250 calories for a pita sandwich.

Compare:

Small Roast Beef Sandwich	230 calories	11 gm fat	519 mg sodium
with			
Deluxe Beef Sandwich	552 calories	28 gm fat	1174 mg sodium

GOOD CHOICES:	Calories	Gm Fat	Mg Sodium
French Dip Sandwich	368	15	1400
Side Salad with	<u>65</u>	<u>5</u>	<u>340</u>
2 Tbsp. Lite Italian Dressing	433	20	1740
or			
6" Roast Beef Sub	345	12	1140

Pizza—Extra Toppings, Extra Calories

It is by no means regrettable that pizza is becoming a more popular fast-food entree. With a tomato sauce base, mozzarella cheese, and a flour-based crust, pizza offers protein, vitamins, and carbohydrates all in one fairly low-fat package. All this is dependent, however, on the choices you make.

As a snack or part of a quick meal, pizza can fit nicely into a well-balanced diet. It's not necessarily a low-calorie food, but with its calories it also contributes very respectably to nutrition. On average, a serving has about 20 grams of protein—more than one-third of the RDA for most adults.

Cheese pizza is a great source of calcium—an average of about 400 milligrams per slice, or one-half of the RDA. Meat pizza average 200 milligrams of calcium—35% of the RDA. Pizza is also a good source of some B vitamins (in the crust) and vitamins A and C (tomato sauce and vegetable toppings).

Two slices of a 16-inch cheese pizza have a total of 375 calories, only 24% of which are from fat. But extra cheese, pepperoni, and sausage toppings mean extra fat and calories—as much as 170 calories per slice. On the other hand, thin crust can save you up to 130 calories per slice. To avoid extra sodium, skip the olives and anchovies.

A salad will round out your pizza meal. Many pizza places offer salads or have salad bars. Fresh fruit for dessert will help fill you up, and you will enjoy a great pizza meal without undue damage to your waistline.

Compare:

Pizza, Cheese 2 slices, medium	466 calories	20 gm fat	1060 mg sodium
with			
Pizza, Pepperoni Lovers, 2 slices, medium	640 calories	36 gm fat	1898 mg sodium

GOOD CHOICES:	Calories	Gm Fat	Mg Sodium
Cheese Pizza 2 slices, 16"	376	10	483
Salad with Low-Cal Italian Dressing	<u>95</u> 471	<u>5</u> 15	<u>340</u> 823
or			
Veggie Lovers 2 slices, 16"	384	16	1102

Potatoes—Plain, Baked Potatoes—A Great Choice

When it comes to potatoes, plain and baked are the best. They are nourishing, filling, and virtually free of fat and sodium.

But all this goodness goes awry when the toppings are added. A plain, large potato provides 240 to 300 calories and a trace of fat. Cheese sauces, bacon, sour cream, and other toppings can increase the fat level by 30 grams (5 to 6 teaspoons) and the calories to 600. A deluxe, superstuffed baked potato with sour cream, butter, bacon, and cheese has 648 calories and more than 7 teaspoons of fat.

Choose a plain, baked potato for lunch or dinner. When combined with a salad and topped with 1/4 cup cottage cheese or one to two tablespoons of grated Swiss, cheddar, or Parmesan cheese, a baked potato becomes a complete meal. Add vegetables instead of high-fat toppings and you save the equivalent of 8 pats of butter. With the calories saved you can even order a plain hamburger!

Other types of potatoes call for other measures. Go easy on the french fries if you are trying to cut calories. Split an order with someone else or, better yet, get a plain, baked potato. If the choice is between mashed potatoes and french fries, get mashed. Even with gravy, they're still lower in fat and calories. If the fries are just too tempting, limit them to a once-in-awhile treat. If it's between fries or onion rings, know that breading makes onion rings higher in fat and calories than french fries.

Compare:

Baked Potato, Plain *with*	300 calories	trace fat	20 mg sodium
Superstuffed Potato	648 calories	38 gm fat	600 mg sodium

GOOD CHOICE:	Calories	Gm Fat	Mg Sodium
Plain Baked Potato	300	tr	20
Chili Topping	190	2	670
	490	2	690

Tacos, Tostadas, and Chili—Choices That Add Fiber

Tacos and tostadas are often excellent choices. Go for bean burritos, soft tacos, or other non-fried items. Spice them to your taste. To keep the fat and calories down, go easy on the cheese, and pass on the sour cream and guacamole. Pile on extra salsa and tomatoes instead.

Chili blows the typical "greasy-spoon" reputation. Chili and several restaurant roast beef sandwiches are just about the only fast-food, red-meat dishes that get less than 30% of their calories from fat. Even a large bowl of chili has only 300 calories and 12 grams of fat.

Beans are one of the best sources of fiber, making chili with beans and baked beans good choices. At the salad bar, choose kidney beans, garbanzo beans, and fruit for added fiber.

Compare:

Chicken Soft Taco	213 calories	10 gm fat	615 mg sodium
with			
Burrito Supreme	422 calories	19 gm fat	952 mg sodium

GOOD CHOICES:	Calories	Gm Fat	Mg Sodium
Chili, large	290	9	1000
Bread Sticks, 4	70	1	120
	360	10	1120
or			
Bean Burrito	359	11	922
or			
Taco, 2	368	22	548
Taco Sauce	2	tr	126
	370	22	674

Salad—A Complement to Any Fast-Food Meal

Salad bars offer a healthful alternative to high-fat sandwiches. But skip the prepared salads (potato, pasta, and so on) and go easy on the dressing. Use of reduced- or low-calorie dressings over regular dressing cuts the calories by at least half.

A large salad containing a variety of vegetables, 1/2 cup of cottage cheese, and reduced-calorie salad dressing has less than 250 calories. However, by adding just one tablespoon of regular dressing, some bacon bits, and 1/4 cup macaroni or potato salad, you increase the calories to 500. Adding coleslaw (1/2 cup, 90 calories), sunflower seeds, and raisins (1/4 cup, 180 calories) adds even more calories.

Compare:

Chef Salad, with Reduced-Calorie Dressing	208 calories	9 gm fat	968 mg sodium
with			
Taco Salad	822 calories	57 gm fat	1368 mg sodium

GOOD CHOICES:	Calories	Gm Fat	Mg Sodium
Seafood Salad	380	31	980
Soda Crackers, 6	75	2	240
	455	33	1220
or			
Chicken Salad Plate	291	19	854
or			
Garden Spot Salad Bar	29	tr	20
Reduced-Calorie Dressing	50	4	340
Cottage Cheese	120	4	500
Bread Stick	130	3	250
	329	11	1110

Fast-Food Beverages—Sources of Hidden Sugar and Fat

The most popular beverage choices at fast-food restaurants are the shakes and soft drinks, hidden sources of sugar and fat. Drink diet beverages, low-fat milk, fruit juice, or water to save calories. Low-fat milk provides more protein and calcium per calorie than a fast-food shake. Fruit juices are high in vitamin C and are good alternatives to higher-calorie sodas and shakes. Other good choices are no-cal coffee, tea, diet sodas, and—the best of all beverage choices—water.

Compare:

Fruit Juice, 6 oz	90 calories	0 gm fat	0 mg sodium
with			
Chocolate Shake, 12 oz	451 calories	12 gm fat	341 gm sodium

GOOD CHOICES:	Calories	Gm Fat	Mg Sodium
2% Lowfat Milk	121	5	122
Diet Soft Drinks	2	0	21

For Dessert—Fresh Fruit, Always A Great Choice

Many fast-food desserts are high in fat and calories, so one option is to satisfy yourself by bringing fresh fruit from home. Try eating your "dessert" fruit first; it's a creative way to curb your appetite and avoid overeating.

Low- or non-fat frozen yogurt (only 80 calories per 1/3 cup with minimal fat) or a small ice-cream cone can also satisfy your sweet tooth with little damage.

Ices, sorbets, and sherbets generally have less fat and fewer calories than ice cream and gelato. Frozen yogurt, ice milk, or lower-calorie ice creams are better health buys—all save calories.

To perk up plain ice cream or yogurt and still save some calories, ask for chocolate sprinkles (about 34 calories per 1/4 ounce) and skip the hot fudge, other sauces, nuts, and whipped toppings.

Compare:

Soft Serve Cone, Regular size	230 calories	7 gm fat	95 mg sodium
with			
Heath Blizzard, Regular size	820 calories	36 gm fat	410 mg sodium

GOOD CHOICES:	Calories	Gm Fat	Mg Sodium
DQ Sandwich	140	4	135
or			
Chocolate Chip Cookie	130	4	95
or			
Cool Twist Cone, 4 oz	180	4	85

Breakfast—Start The Day With Care

Making fast-food choices for lunch or dinner can be easier than choosing for breakfast. Morning food options tend to be very heavy in fat, calories, and cholesterol. For instance, egg dishes with bacon, sausage, or ham have from 250 to 525 milligrams of cholesterol. The National Cholesterol Education Program recommends that we eat no more than 300 milligrams of cholesterol daily. Counterbalance a fast-food egg breakfast by cutting back on eggs the rest of the week.

Sausage versions of breakfast sandwiches are also generally higher in fat and calories. A sausage and egg biscuit, hash brown potatoes, and a large orange juice contribute 820 calories, 49 grams of fat, and 1475 milligrams of sodium.

Try to order breakfast sandwiches on virtually fat-free English muffins, bagels, or hamburger buns. Breakfast biscuits contain 500 to 700 calories, 30 to 35 grams of fat, and more than 1000 milligrams of sodium. Even plain croissants are high in fat—equal to about four pats of butter.

Rather than a breakfast sandwich, start your day with plain muffins, English muffins, bagels, or toast. Request no butter and use low-sugar jam or jelly instead. Add fruit juice and low-fat or skim milk.

A substantial breakfast of one scrambled egg and an English muffin contains only 366 calories, 17 grams of fat, and 575 milligrams of sodium. Other choices are bagels with cottage cheese and applesauce, cereal with fresh fruit and milk, yogurt and a banana, an apple with peanut butter, or a muffin and juice.

A surprisingly good breakfast option is pancakes without butter. They have less fat than croissants and are relatively cholesterol-free. Bring your own diet jam, jelly, or syrup.

Compare:

Egg Muffin	280 calories	11 gm fat	710 mg sodium
with			
Big Country Breakfast Sausage	850 calories	57 gm fat	1900 mg sodium
or			
English Muffin with Margarine	190 calories	5 gm fat	280 mg sodium
with			
Cinnamon Roll	460 calories	18 gm fat	230 mg sodium

GOOD CHOICES:	Calories	Gm Fat	Mg Sodium
Pancakes, 3	280	2	890
or			
Breakfast Burrito, 1	280	17	580
or			
Egg Omelette Sandwich	312	15	696

Summing It All Up

Today many fast-food restaurants offer salad bars, low-calorie salad dressings, soups, baked potatoes, baked fish, grilled chicken sandwiches, diet soft drinks, and low-fat milk that can help the health-conscious consumer, as well as the person with diabetes, limit calories, fat, and sodium in a fast-food meal.

Make wise food choices. If you have fast foods for one meal, try to balance what you eat the rest of the day. Even the harshest critic of fast food has to admit it's convenient. You don't have to go far or wait long to get fast food. This can be a major advantage, especially if you have limited time to eat.

If You Have Diabetes

People with diabetes will no doubt at times find it convenient or necessary to eat fast foods. When you do, use the guidelines in this book to help you make wise decisions. Know your meal plan. You'll need to choose foods that fit into your available choices for meals and snacks.

Avoid high-fat, high-sugar, and high-sodium foods. Set your goals for approximately 20 to 25 grams of fat, and not more than 1000 milligrams of sodium (1/2 teaspoon of salt) per meal. If weight is a concern, pay special attention to caloric values.

You may need to supplement a fast-food meal with some fruit and/or milk. Nutritional adequacy can be assured by eating a variety of vegetables, fruits, low-fat milk, and whole-grain foods in the rest of your meals and snacks during the day.

By knowing the nutritional value of fast-food items, you can choose foods that will be consistent with your meal plan. Food values in fast-food chains may be easier to predict than some expensive gourmet restaurants. Studies of the leading chains show remarkable uniformity in portion sizes and nutrition value of their foods.

Fast-Food Nutrient and Exchange Values

The fast-food restaurant lists are divided into three sections: 1) menu items, nutritive values, and suggested exchanges; 2) menu items, nutritive values, and suggested exchanges for foods recommended for occasional use only due to their sugar content; 3) menu items and nutritive values for foods that are not recommended for use because of the large amounts of added sugar they contain.

You may find that some foods on the lists may not fit into your meal plan. They may contain too many calories or too much fat and, as a result, the exchange values may be greater than the number you have available in your meal plan. A "冒" symbol has been placed in the margin for items with more than 2 fat exchanges per serving. Sodium values in milligrams per serving are included to help you regulate sodium consumption. A "⌁" symbol has been placed in the margins for items with more than 800 milligrams of sodium. A "🦷" symbol appears next to foods that contain moderate to high amounts of sugar.

We've listed nutritive information for many fast-food establishments found in the US and Canada, including calories, grams of carbohydrate, protein, fat, saturated fat and cholesterol, milligrams of sodium, and suggested exchange values. Some of the nutritive values for food items are based on actual laboratory analysis and some were calculated from nutrient composition tables. The values listed are averages and may vary from restaurant to restaurant.

This book is designed to not only alert you to the nutritive and exchange values of food items, but to help you make wise food choices and still enjoy eating at fast-food restaurants. Good luck!

Marion J. Franz, M.S., R.D., C.D.E.
International Diabetes Center

Products	SERVING SIZE	CALORIES	CARBO-HYDRATE (gm)	PROTEIN (gm)	FAT (gm)	SAT. FAT (gm)	CHOLES-TEROL (mg)	SODIUM (mg)	Exchanges

ARBY'S

Sandwiches

Products	SERVING SIZE	CALORIES	CARBO-HYDRATE (gm)	PROTEIN (gm)	FAT (gm)	SAT. FAT (gm)	CHOLES-TEROL (mg)	SODIUM (mg)	Exchanges
Junior Roast Beef	1 (3.1 oz.)	233	23	12	11	4	22	519	1½ starch, 1½ med. fat meat
Regular Roast Beef	1 (5.5 oz.)	383	35	22	18	7	43	936	2 starch, 2 med. fat meat, 1½ fat
Beef n Cheddar	1 (7 oz.)	508	43	25	27	8	52	1166	3 starch, 2½ med. fat meat, 2 fat
Bac n Cheddar Deluxe	1 (8 oz.)	512	39	22	32	8	38	1094	2½ starch, 2 med. fat meat, 4 fat
Giant Roast Beef	1 (8.5 oz.)	544	46	33	26	11	72	1433	3 starch, 3 med. fat meat, 2 fat
Super Roast Beef	1 (9 oz.)	552	54	24	28	8	43	1174	3½ starch, 2 med. fat meat, 3 fat
Philly Beef 'N Swiss	1 (7 oz.)	467	38	24	25	10	53	1144	2½ starch, 2½ med. fat meat, 2 fat
French Dip	1 (5.4 oz.)	368	35	22	15	6	43	1018	2 starch, 2 med. fat meat, 1 fat
French Dip 'N Swiss	1 (6.3 oz.)	429	35	29	19	9	67	1438	2 starch, 3 med. fat meat, 1 fat
Arby Q	1 (6.7 oz.)	389	48	18	15	6	29	1268	3 starch, 1 med. fat meat, 2 fat
Chicken Breast Fillet Sandwich	1 (7.2 oz.)	445	42	22	23	3	45	958	3 starch, 2 med. fat meat, 2 fat
Roast Chicken Club	1 (8.4 oz.)	503	37	30	27	7	46	1143	2½ starch, 3 med. fat meat, 2 fat
Chicken Cordon Bleu	1 (8 oz.)	518	52	30	27	5	92	1463	3 starch, 3 med. fat meat, 2 fat
Grilled Chicken Deluxe	1 (8.1 oz.)	430	42	24	20	4	44	901	2½ starch, 2½ med. fat meat, 1 fat
Grilled Chicken Barbeque	1 (7.1 oz.)	386	47	24	13	4	43	1002	3 starch, 2 med. fat meat
Hot Ham n Cheese Sandwich	1 (6 oz.)	355	35	25	14	5	55	1400	2 starch, 3 med. fat meat
Fish Fillet Sandwich	1 (7.8 oz.)	526	50	23	27	7	44	872	3 starch, 2 med. fat meat, 3 fat

Ｂ = More than 2 fat exchanges per serving   ☀ = More than 800 milligrams sodium   ♣ = High amounts of sugar

Products	SERVING SIZE	CALORIES	CARBO-HYDRATE (gm)	PROTEIN (gm)	FAT (gm)	SAT. FAT (gm)	CHOLES-TEROL (mg)	SODIUM (mg)	Exchanges
Italian Sub	1 (10.5 oz.)	671	47	34	39	13	69	2062	3 starch, 3½ med. fat meat, 4 fat
Roast Beef Sub	1 (10.8 oz.)	623	47	38	32	12	73	1847	3 starch, 4 med. fat meat, 2 fat
Tuna Sub	1 (10 oz.)	663	50	34	37	8	43	1342	3 starch, 3½ med. fat meat, 4 fat
Turkey Sub	1 (9.7 oz.)	486	46	33	19	5	51	2033	3 starch, 3½ med. fat meat

Light Menu

Products	SERVING SIZE	CALORIES	CARBO-HYDRATE (gm)	PROTEIN (gm)	FAT (gm)	SAT. FAT (gm)	CHOLES-TEROL (mg)	SODIUM (mg)	Exchanges
Light Roast Chicken Deluxe	1 (6.8 oz.)	276	33	24	7	2	33	777	2 starch, 2½ lean meat
Light Roast Turkey Deluxe	1 (6.8 oz.)	260	33	20	6	2	33	1262	2 starch, 2 lean meat
Light Roast Beef Deluxe	1 (6.4 oz.)	294	33	18	10	4	42	826	2 starch, 2 med. meat

Potatoes

Products	SERVING SIZE	CALORIES	CARBO-HYDRATE (gm)	PROTEIN (gm)	FAT (gm)	SAT. FAT (gm)	CHOLES-TEROL (mg)	SODIUM (mg)	Exchanges
Baked Potato, Plain	1 (8.5 oz.)	240	50	6	2	0	0	58	3 starch
Baked Potato, with Butter, Sour Cream	1 (11 oz.)	463	53	8	25	12	40	203	3 starch, 5 fat
Broccoli 'N Cheddar Baked Potato	1 (12 oz.)	417	55	11	18	7	22	361	3 starch 1 vegetable, 1 high fat meat, 2 fat
Deluxe Baked Potato	1 (12.3 oz.)	621	59	17	36	18	58	605	4 starch, 1 high fat meat, 5 fat
Mushroom 'N Cheese Baked Potato	1 (12.3 oz.)	515	58	15	27	6	47	923	4 starch, 1 high fat meat, 3 fat
French Fries	1 (2.5 oz.)	246	30	2	13	3	0	114	2 starch, 2 fat
Potato Cakes	1 (3 oz.)	204	20	2	12	2	0	397	1½ starch, 2 fat
Curly Fries	1 (3.5 oz.)	337	43	4	18	7	0	167	3 starch, 3 fat
Cheddar Fries	1 (5 oz.)	399	46	6	22	9	9	443	3 starch, 4 fat

Salads

Products	SERVING SIZE	CALORIES	CARBO-HYDRATE (gm)	PROTEIN (gm)	FAT (gm)	SAT. FAT (gm)	CHOLES-TEROL (mg)	SODIUM (mg)	Exchanges
Garden Salad	1 (11.6 oz.)	117	11	7	5	3	12	134	2 vegetable 1 fat

Products	SERVING SIZE	CALORIES	CARBO-HYDRATE (gm)	PROTEIN (gm)	FAT (gm)	SAT. FAT (gm)	CHOLES-TEROL (mg)	SODIUM (mg)	Exchanges
Roast Chicken Salad	1 (14 oz.)	204	24	12	7	3	43	508	1 starch, 2 vegetable, 1 med. fat meat
Chef Salad	1 (14.5 oz.)	205	13	19	10	4	126	796	2 vegetable 2 med. fat meat
Side Salad	1 (5.3 oz.)	25	4	2	tr	-	0	30	1 vegetable
Salad Dressings/Condiments									
日 Honey French Dressing	1 (2 oz.)	322	22	tr	27	4	0	486	1 starch, 5 fat
🌡 Light Italian Dressing	1 (2 oz.)	23	3	0	1	-	0	1110	Free
日 Thousand Island Dressing	1 (2 oz.)	298	10	tr	29	4	24	493	½ starch 6 fat
日 Blue Cheese Dressing	1 (2 oz.)	295	2	2	31	6	50	489	6 fat
日 Buttermilk Ranch Dressing	1 (2 oz.)	349	2	tr	39	6	6	471	8 fat
Croutons	1 (.5 oz.)	59	8	2	2	tr	1	155	½ starch
Arby's Sauce	1 (.5 oz.)	15	3	tr	tr	0	113	Free	
Horsey Sauce	1 (.5 oz.)	55	3	tr	5	-	105	1 fat	
Ketchup	1 (.5 oz.)	16	4	tr	0	0	0	143	Free
Mustard	1 (.5 oz.)	11	tr	tr	tr	0	0	160	Free
Mayonnaise P.C.	1 (.5 oz.)	90	0	0	10	1	0	75	2 fat
Soups									
🌡 Boston Clam Chowder	1 (8 oz.)	193	18	8	10	5	26	1032	1 starch, 2 fat
🌡 Cream of Broccoli Soup	1 (8 oz.)	166	18	8	7	4	24	1050	1 starch, 2 fat
🌡 Lumberjack Mixed Vegetable Soup	1 (8 oz.)	89	13	2	3	2	4	1075	1 starch
🌡 Old Fashioned Chicken Noodle	1 (8 oz.)	99	15	6	2	-	25	929	1 starch
🌡 Potato with Bacon Soup	1 (8 oz.)	184	20	6	9	4	20	1068	1 starch, 2 fat

日 = More than 2 fat exchanges per serving   🌡 = More than 800 milligrams sodium   ❦ = High amounts of sugar

Products	SERVING SIZE	CALORIES	CARBO-HYDRATE (gm)	PROTEIN (gm)	FAT (gm)	SAT. FAT (gm)	CHOLES-TEROL (mg)	SODIUM (mg)	Exchanges
✸ Wisconsin Cheese Soup	1 (8 oz.)	281	20	9	18	9	32	1084	1 starch, 1 high fat meat, 2 fat
Breakfast Items									
🅑 Toastix	1 (3.5 oz.)	420	43	8	25	5	20	440	3 starch, 4 fat
🌰 Maple Syrup	1 (1.5 oz.)	120	29	0	tr	0	0	52	2 starch or 2 fruit
Cinnamon Nut Danish	1 (3.5 oz.)	360	60	6	11	1	0	105	4 starch 2 fat
🅑 Plain Biscuit	1 (2.9 oz.)	280	34	6	15	3	0	730	2 starch 3 fat
🅑 ✸ Bacon Biscuit	1 (3.1 oz.)	318	35	7	18	5	8	904	2 starch 4 fat
🅑 ✸ Sausage Biscuit	1 (4.2 oz.)	460	35	12	32	10	60	1000	2 starch, 1 high fat meat, 5 fat
✸ Ham Biscuit	1 (4.4 oz.)	323	34	13	17	4	21	1169	2 starch, 1 med. fat meat. 2 fat
🅑 Plain Croissant	1 (2.2)	260	28	6	16	10	49	300	2 starch, 3 fat
🅑 Bacon/Egg Croissant	1 (4.3 oz.)	430	29	17	30	15	245	720	2 starch, 2 med. fat meat, 3 fat
✸ Ham/Cheese Croissant	1 (4.2 oz.)	345	29	16	21	12	90	939	2 starch, 1½ med. fat meat, 2 fat
🅑 ✸ Mushroom/Cheese Croissant	1 (5.2 oz.)	493	34	13	38	15	116	935	2 starch, 1 med. fat meat, 6 fat
🅑 ✸ Sausage/Egg Croissant	1 (5 oz.)	519	29	18	39	19	271	632	2 starch, 2 med. fat meat, 5 fat
🅑 ✸ Ham Platter	1 (9.1 oz.)	518	45	24	26	8	374	1177	3 starch, 2 med. fat meat, 3 fat
🅑 ✸ Sausage Platter	1 (8.4 oz.)	640	46	21	41	13	406	861	3 starch, 2 med. fat meat, 6 fat
🅑 Egg Platter	1 (7.1 oz.)	460	45	15	24	7	346	591	3 starch, 1 med. fat meat, 4 fat
🅑 ✸ Bacon Platter	1 (7.8 oz.)	593	51	22	33	9	458	880	3½ starch, 2 med. fat meat, 4 fat
Blueberry Muffin	1 (2.7 oz.)	240	40	4	7	1	22	200	2½ starch, 1 fat

Products	SERVING SIZE	CALORIES	CARBO-HYDRATE (gm)	PROTEIN (gm)	FAT (gm)	SAT. FAT (gm)	CHOLES-TEROL (mg)	SODIUM (mg)	Exchanges
Orange Juice	1 (6 oz.)	82	20	1	0	0	0	2	1 fruit
♥ Hot Chocolate	1 (8 oz.)	110	23	2	1	tr	0	120	1½ starch

OCCASIONAL USE

Products	SERVING SIZE	CALORIES	CARBO-HYDRATE (gm)	PROTEIN (gm)	FAT (gm)	SAT. FAT (gm)	CHOLES-TEROL (mg)	SODIUM (mg)	Exchanges
Apple Turnover	1 (3 oz.)	303	28	4	18	7	0	178	2 starch, 3 fat
Cherry Turnover	1 (3 oz.)	280	25	4	18	5	0	200	2 starch, 3 fat
Blueberry Turnovor	1 (3 oz.)	320	32	3	19	6	0	240	2 starch, 3½ fat
Cheese Cake	1 (3 oz.)	306	21	5	23	7	95	220	1½ starch, 4 fat
Chocolate Chip Cookie	1 (1 oz.)	130	17	2	4	2	0	95	1 starch, 1 fat
♥ Vanilla Shake	1 (11 oz.)	330	46	11	12	4	32	281	3 starch, 2 fat

NOT RECOMMENDED FOR USE

Products	SERVING SIZE	CALORIES	CARBO-HYDRATE (gm)	PROTEIN (gm)	FAT (gm)	SAT. FAT (gm)	CHOLES-TEROL (mg)	SODIUM (mg)	Exchanges
♥ Chocolate Shake	1 (12 oz.)	451	76	10	12	3	36	341	
♥ Jamocha Shake	1 (11.5 oz.)	368	59	9	11	3	35	262	
Peanut Butter Cup Polar Swirl	1 (11.6 oz.)	517	61	14	24	8	34	386	
Oreo Polar Swirl	1 (11.6 oz.)	482	66	11	20	10	35	521	
Snickers Polar Swirl	1 (11.6 oz.)	511	73	12	19	7	33	351	
Heath Polar Swirl	1 (11.6 oz.)	543	76	11	22	5	39	346	
Butterfinger Polar	1 (11.6 oz.)	457	62	12	18	8	28	318	

BASKIN-ROBBINS

OCCASIONAL USE

Deluxe Ice Cream

Products	SERVING SIZE	CALORIES	CARBO-HYDRATE (gm)	PROTEIN (gm)	FAT (gm)	SAT. FAT (gm)	CHOLES-TEROL (mg)	SODIUM (mg)	Exchanges
Vanilla	1 Regular Scoop	240	24	4	14	NA	52	115	1½ starch, 3 fat

⊟ = More than 2 fat exchanges per serving   ⚕ = More than 800 milligrams sodium   ♥ = High amounts of sugar

Products	SERVING SIZE	CALORIES	CARBO-HYDRATE (gm)	PROTEIN (gm)	FAT (gm)	SAT. FAT (gm)	CHOLES-TEROL (mg)	SODIUM (mg)	Exchanges
Very Berry Strawberry	1 Regular Scoop	220	30	3	10	NA	30	95	2 starch, 2 fat
World Class Chocolate	1 Regular Scoop	280	35	5	14	NA	36	145	2 starch, 3 fat
Sherbet & Ices									
Daiquiri Ice	1 Regular Scoop	140	35	0	0	NA	0	15	2 starch or 2 fruit
Rainbow Shebet	1 Regular Scoop	160	34	1	2	NA	6	85	2 starch or 2 fruit
International Creams									
Chocolate Raspberry Truffle	1 Regular Scoop	310	35	4	17	NA	45	115	2 starch, 3½ fat
Sundae Bar									
Jamaica Almond Fudge	1 bar	300	41	5	13	NA	24	86	3 starch, 2 fat
Sundae Bar Light									
Chocolate with Caramel Ribbon	1 bar	150	24	3	5	NA	11	75	1½ starch, 1 fat
Vanilla with Chocolate Ribbon	1 bar	150	26	3	4	NA	10	75	1½ starch, 1 fat
Premium Frozen Yogurt Bars									
Dutch Chocolate Chip	1	260	28	4	14	NA	7	94	2 starch, 3 fat
Praline Vanilla	1	250	26	4	14	NA	7	76	1½ starch, 3 fat
Chilly Burgers	1	240	32	4	11	NA	29	130	2 starch, 2 fat
Tiny Toon Adventures Ice Cream Bars									
Vanilla	1	210	18	3	14	NA	18	35	1 starch, 3 fat
Mint Chocolate Chip	1	230	19	3	15	NA	17	35	1 starch, 3 fat

Products	SERVING SIZE	CALORIES	CARBO-HYDRATE (gm)	PROTEIN (gm)	FAT (gm)	SAT. FAT (gm)	CHOLES-TEROL (mg)	SODIUM (mg)	Exchanges
Tiny Toon Adventures Toonwiches									
♥ ◻ Vanilla	1	340	45	5	16	NA	34	65	3 starch, 3 fat
♥ ◻ Chocolate	1	330	46	4	14	NA	33	105	3 starch, 3 fat
Cones									
♥ Sugar	1	60	11	1	1	NA	0	45	1 starch or 1 fruit
♥ Waffle	1	140	28	3	2	NA	0	5	2 starch
Fat Free Ice Cream									
♥ Chocolate Vanilla Twist	½ cup	100	21	4	0	NA	0	60	1½ starch
♥ Just Peachy	½ cup	100	22	3	0	NA	0	60	1½ starch
Sugar Free Ice Cream									
Jamoca Swiss Almond	½ cup	90	19	3	2	NA	4	100	1 starch
Strawberry	½ cup	80	17	2	1	NA	3	70	1 starch
Light Ice Cream									
Praline Cream	½ cup	130	17	3	6	NA	11	85	1 starch, 1 fat
Strawberry Royal	½ cup	110	19	2	3	NA	9	120	1 starch, ½ fat
Frozen Yogurt									
♥ Low-Fat Strawberry	½ cup	120	24	4	1	NA	5	40	1½ starch
♥ Non-Fat Strawberry	½ cup	110	24	3	0	NA	0	40	1½ starch
Truly Free Frozen Yogurt Wild Cherry	½ cup	70	16	4	0	NA	0	15	1 starch
♥ Soft-Serve Sorbet Strawberry	½ cup	100	20	0	0	NA	0	20	1 ½ starch or 1½ fruit

◻ = More than 2 fat exchanges per serving   ☩ = More than 800 milligrams sodium   ♥ = High amounts of sugar

Products	SERVING SIZE	CALORIES	CARBO-HYDRATE (gm)	PROTEIN (gm)	FAT (gm)	SAT. FAT (gm)	CHOLES-TEROL (mg)	SODIUM (mg)	Exchanges

BURGER KING

Sandwiches

Products	SERVING SIZE	CALORIES	CARBO-HYDRATE (gm)	PROTEIN (gm)	FAT (gm)	SAT. FAT (gm)	CHOLES-TEROL (mg)	SODIUM (mg)	Exchanges
Hamburger	1 (3.6 oz.)	260	28	14	10	4	30	500	2 starch, 2 med. fat meat
Cheeseburger	1 (4 oz.)	300	28	16	14	6	45	660	2 starch, 2 med. fat meat, 1 fat
Whopper Sandwich	1 (9.5 oz.)	570	46	27	31	12	80	870	3 starch, 3 med. fat meat, 3 fat
Whopper w/Cheese	1 (10.3 oz.)	660	48	32	38	14	105	1190	3 starch, 4 med. fat meat, 3 fat
Whopper Jr.	1 (4.7 oz.)	300	29	14	15	5	35	500	2 starch, 1½ med. fat meat, 1 fat
Whopper Jr. w/Cheese	1 (5 oz.)	350	30	16	19	7	45	650	2 starch, 2 med. fat meat, 1 fat
Double Whopper	1 (12.3 oz.)	800	46	46	48	18	160	940	3 starch, 5 med. fat meat, 4 fat
Double Whopper with Cheese	1 (13.2 oz.)	890	48	51	55	22	185	1250	3 starch, 6 med. fat meat, 5 fat
Bacon Double Cheeseburger	1 (5.3 oz.)	470	26	30	28	13	100	800	2 starch, 3 med. fat meat, 2 fat
Bacon Double Cheeseburger Deluxe	1 (6.5 oz.)	530	28	30	33	14	100	860	2 starch, 3 med. fat meat, 3 fat
Double Cheeseburger	1 (5.6 oz.)	450	29	27	25	12	90	840	2 starch, 3 med. fat meat, 2 fat
BK Broiler Chicken Sandwich	1 (5.4 oz.)	280	29	20	10	2	50	770	2 starch, 2 med. fat meat
Chicken Sandwich	1 (8 oz.)	620	57	26	32	7	45	1430	4 starch, 2 med. fat meat, 4 fat
Chicken Tenders	6 pieces	236	14	16	13	3	38	541	1 starch, 2 med. fat meat
Ocean Catch Fish Filet Sandwich	1 (5.8 oz.)	450	33	16	28	7	30	760	2 starch, 2 med. fat meat, 3 fat

Side Orders

Products	SERVING SIZE	CALORIES	CARBO-HYDRATE (gm)	PROTEIN (gm)	FAT (gm)	SAT. FAT (gm)	CHOLES-TEROL (mg)	SODIUM (mg)	Exchanges
Chef Salad w/out Salad Dressing	1 (9.6 oz.)	178	7	17	9	4	103	568	1 vegetable, 2 med. fat meat

Products	SERVING SIZE	CALORIES	CARBO-HYDRATE (gm)	PROTEIN (gm)	FAT (gm)	SAT. FAT (gm)	CHOLES-TEROL (mg)	SODIUM (mg)	Exchanges
Chicken Salad w/out Salad Dressing	1 (9 oz.)	142	8	20	4	1	49	443	1 vegetable, 2 lean meat
Garden Salad w/out Salad Dressing	1 (7.8 oz.)	95	8	6	5	3	15	125	1 vegetable, 1 med. fat meat
Side Salad w/out Salad Dressing	1 (4.8 oz.)	25	5	1	0	0	0	27	1 vegetable
▤ Onion Rings	1 (3.4 oz.)	339	38	5	19	5	0	628	2½ starch, 3 fat
▤ French Fries (medium, salted)	1 (4 oz.)	372	43	5	20	5	0	238	3 starch, 3 fat

Salad Dressings/Condiments

Products	SERVING SIZE	CALORIES	CARBO-HYDRATE (gm)	PROTEIN (gm)	FAT (gm)	SAT. FAT (gm)	CHOLES-TEROL (mg)	SODIUM (mg)	Exchanges
BK Broiler Sauce	1 (.4 oz.)	37	1	0	4	1	5	74	1 fat
Bull's Eye Barbecue Sauce	1 (.5 oz.)	22	5	0	0	0	0	47	Free
▤ Mayonnaise Reduced Calorie	1 (1 oz.)	130	3	0	13	2	0	150	2½ fat
Tartar Sauce	1 (1 oz.)	100	4	0	10	2	0	220	2 fat
▤ Thousand Island Dressing	1 (2.2 oz.)	290	15	1	26	5	36	403	1 starch, 5 fat
▤ Blue Cheese Salad Dressing	1 (2 oz.)	300	2	3	32	7	58	512	6 fat
▤ French Dressing	1 (2.2 oz.)	290	23	0	22	3	0	400	1 starch, 5 fat
▤ Ranch Dressing	1 (2 oz.)	350	4	1	37	7	20	316	8 fat
Light Italian Dressing	1 (2 oz.)	30	6	0	1	0	0	710	½ fat
A.M. Express Dip	1 (1 oz.)	84	21	0	0	0	0	18	1 starch
Honey Dipping Sauce	1 (1 oz.)	91	23	0	0	0	0	12	1½ starch
▤ Ranch Dipping Sauce	1 (1 oz.)	171	2	0	18	3	0	208	4 fat
Barbecue Sauce	1 (1 oz.)	36	9	0	0	0	0	397	½ starch
Sweet & Sour Dipping Sauce	1 (1 oz.)	45	11	0	0	0	0	52	½ starch

▤ = More than 2 fat exchanges per serving   ☀ = More than 800 milligrams sodium   ✿ = High amounts of sugar

Products	SERVING SIZE	CALORIES	CARBO-HYDRATE (gm)	PROTEIN (gm)	FAT (gm)	SAT. FAT (gm)	CHOLES-TEROL (mg)	SODIUM (mg)	Exchanges
Breakfast Items									
Bacon, Egg, Cheese Croissanwich	1 (4 oz.)	353	19	16	23	8	230	780	1 starch, 2 med. fat meat, 3 fat
Sausage, Egg, Cheese Croissanwich	1 (5.6 oz.)	534	22	21	40	14	258	985	1½ starch, 2½ med. fat meat, 5 fat
Ham, Egg, Cheese Croissanwich	1 (5 oz.)	351	20	19	22	7	236	1373	1½ starch, 2 med. fat meat, 2 fat
Breakfast Buddy with Sausage, Egg, Cheese	1 (3 oz.)	255	15	11	16	6	127	492	1 starch, 1 med. fat meat, 2 fat
French Toast Sticks	1 (5 oz.)	440	60	4	27	7	0	490	4 starch, 4 fat
Hash Browns	1 (2.5 oz.)	213	25	2	12	3	0	318	1½ starch, 2 fat
Blueberry Mini Muffins	1 (3.3 oz.)	292	37	4	14	3	72	244	2½ starch, 2 fat
Orange Juice	1 (6.5 oz.)	82	20	1	0	0	0	2	1½ fruit
OCCASIONAL USE									
Apple Pie	1 (4.5 oz.)	320	45	3	14	4	0	420	2 starch, 1 fruit, 2 fat
Cherry Pie	1 (4.5 oz.)	360	55	4	13	4	0	200	2½ starch, 1 fruit, 2 fat
Lemon Pie	1 (3.2 oz.)	290	49	6	8	3	35	105	3 starch, 1 fat
Snickers Ice Cream Bar	1 (2 oz.)	220	20	5	14	7	15	65	1½ starch, 2½ fat
Vanilla Shake	1 (10 oz.)	334	51	9	10	6	33	213	3 starch, 2 fat
Chocolate Shake	1 (10 oz.)	326	49	9	10	6	31	198	3 starch, 2 fat
NOT RECOMMENDED FOR USE									
Chocolate Shake (syrup added)	1 (11 oz.)	409	68	10	11	6	33	248	
Strawberry Shake (syrup added)	1 (11 oz.)	394	66	9	10	6	33	230	

CARL'S JR.

Sandwiches

Products	SERVING SIZE	CALORIES	CARBO-HYDRATE (gm)	PROTEIN (gm)	FAT (gm)	SAT. FAT (gm)	CHOLES-TEROL (mg)	SODIUM (mg)	Exchanges
🄱🏌 Famous Star Hamburger	1 (8.6 oz.)	610	42	26	38	13	50	890	3 starch, 3 med. fat meat, 3 fat
🄱🏌 Super Star Hamburger	1 (11.25 oz.)	820	41	43	53	24	105	1210	3 starch, 5 med. fat meat, 5 fat
🄱🏌 Western Bacon Cheeseburger	1 (8.2 oz.)	730	59	34	39	20	90	1490	4 starch, 3 med. fat meat, 4 fat
🄱🏌 Double Western Bacon Cheeseburger	1 (11.6 oz.)	1030	58	56	63	32	145	1810	4 starch, 6 med. fat meat, 6 fat
🏌 Carl's Original Hamburger	1 (6.8 oz.)	460	46	25	20	9	50	810	3 starch, 2 med. fat meat, 2 fat
Hamburger	1 (4.3 oz.)	320	33	17	14	5	35	590	2 starch, 2 med. fat meat
Charbroiler BBQ Chicken Sandwich	1 (11 oz.)	310	34	25	6	2	30	680	2 starch, 3 lean meat
🏌 Charbroiler Chicken Club Sandwich	1 (20 oz.)	570	42	35	29	8	60	1160	3 starch, 4 med. fat meat, 1 fat
🏌 Teriyaki Chicken Sandwich	1 (8.3 oz.)	330	42	28	6	2	55	830	2½ starch, 2½ lean meat
🏌 Santa Fe Chicken Sandwich	1 (7.8 oz.)	540	75	30	13	3	40	1180	5 starch, 2½ lean meat
🏌 Turkey Club Sandwich	1 (9.4 oz.)	530	50	30	23	6	60	2890	3 starch, 3 med. fat meat, 1½ fat
🏌 Roast Beef Deluxe Sandwich	1 9.3 oz.)	540	46	28	26	10	40	1340	3 starch, 3 med. meat, 2 fat
🄱🏌 Roast Beef Club Sandwich	1 (9.5 oz.)	620	48	30	34	11	45	1950	3 starch, 3 med. fat meat, 4 fat
🄱🏌 Carl's Catch Fish Sandwich	1 (7.5 oz.)	560	54	17	30	4	5	1220	3½ starch, 1 med. fat meat, 5 fat

Potatoes/Side Order

Products	SERVING SIZE	CALORIES	CARBO-HYDRATE (gm)	PROTEIN (gm)	FAT (gm)	SAT. FAT (gm)	CHOLES-TEROL (mg)	SODIUM (mg)	Exchanges
🄱🏌 Broccoli & Cheese Potato	1 (15 oz.)	590	60	18	31	11	25	830	4 starch, 1 med. fat meat, 5 fat

🄱 = More than 2 fat exchanges per serving   🏌 = More than 800 milligrams sodium   🍷 = High amounts of sugar

Products	SERVING SIZE	CALORIES	CARBO-HYDRATE (gm)	PROTEIN (gm)	FAT (gm)	SAT. FAT (gm)	CHOLES-TEROL (mg)	SODIUM (mg)	Exchanges
Bacon & Cheese Potato	1 (15 oz.)	730	60	26	43	15	45	1670	4 starch, 2 med. fat meat, 6 fat
Sour Cream & Chive Potato	1 (12 oz.)	470	64	11	19	7	20	180	4 starch, 3½ fat
Cheese Potato	1 (14.6 oz.)	690	70	23	36	15	40	1160	4½ starch, 2 med. fat meat, 4 fat
Lite Potato	1 (10 oz.)	290	60	9	1	0	0	60	4 starch
French Fries (regular size)	1 (4.4 oz.)	420	54	4	20	5	0	200	3½ starch, 3 fat
Zucchini	1 (6 oz.)	390	38	7	23	6	0	1040	2½ starch, 4 fat
Onion Rings	1 (5.3 oz.)	520	63	9	26	6	0	960	4 starch, 5 fat
CrissCut Fries (regular size)	1 (3.2 oz.)	330	27	4	22	3	0	890	2 starch, 4 fat
Chicken Strips (3.7 oz.)	6 pieces	260	11	19	19	5	25	600	1½ starch, 2 med. fat meat, 2 fat
Salsa	1 (1 oz.)	8	2	0	0	0	0	210	Free

Salads/Salad Dressings

Products	SERVING SIZE	CALORIES	CARBO-HYDRATE (gm)	PROTEIN (gm)	FAT (gm)	SAT. FAT (gm)	CHOLES-TEROL (mg)	SODIUM (mg)	Exchanges
Garden Salad To-Go	1 (4.8 oz.)	50	4	3	3	2	5	75	1 vegetable
Chicken Salad To-Go	1 (12 oz.)	200	8	24	8	4	70	300	1 vegetable, 3 lean meat
Italian Dressing	1 oz.	120	1	0	13	2	0	210	3 fat
House Dressing	1 oz.	110	1	1	11	3	10	170	2 fat
Blue Cheese Dressing	1 oz.	150	0	1	15	3	20	250	3 fat
1000 Island Dressing	2 oz.	110	4	0	11	3	5	200	2 fat
Reduced Calorie French Dressing	1 oz.	40	5	0	2	0	0	290	1 fat

Breakfast Items

Products	SERVING SIZE	CALORIES	CARBO-HYDRATE (gm)	PROTEIN (gm)	FAT (gm)	SAT. FAT (gm)	CHOLES-TEROL (mg)	SODIUM (mg)	Exchanges
Orange Juice	1 (9 oz.) Small Size	90	21	2	tr	tr	0	2	1½ fruit
Sunrise Sandwich	1 (4 oz.)	300	31	15	13	6	160	550	2 starch, 2 med. fat meat

Products	SERVING SIZE	CALORIES	CARBO-HYDRATE (gm)	PROTEIN (gm)	FAT (gm)	SAT. FAT (gm)	CHOLES-TEROL (mg)	SODIUM (mg)	Exchanges
⽇ Breakfast Burrito	1 (5.3 oz.)	430	29	22	26	12	285	740	2 starch, 2 med. fat meat, 3 fat
⽇ French Toast Dips (syrup not included)	1 (4.3 oz.)	490	55	8	26	6	40	620	3½ starch, 5 fat
Scrambled Eggs	1 order (2.3 oz.)	120	2	9	9	4	245	105	1 med. fat meat, 1 fat
⽇ ⚕ Hot Cakes w/Margarine (syrup not included)	1 order (6.6 oz.)	510	61	11	24	5	10	950	4 starch, 4 fat
English Muffin w/Margarine	1 (2 oz.)	190	30	6	5	1	0	280	2 starch, 1 fat
Sausage	1 patty (6.7 oz.)	190	0	8	18	5	30	520	1 high fat meat, 2 fat
Bacon	2 strips (.3 oz.)	45	0	3	4	1	5	150	1 fat
⽇ Hashed Brown Nuggets	1 (3.3 oz.)	270	27	3	17	4	5	410	2 starch, 3 fat
Blueberry Muffins	1 (4.2 oz.)	340	61	5	9	1	45	300	4 starch, 1 fat
Bran Muffins	1 (4.8 oz.)	310	52	6	7	0	60	370	3½ starch, 1 fat

OCCASIONAL USE

Products	SERVING SIZE	CALORIES	CARBO-HYDRATE (gm)	PROTEIN (gm)	FAT (gm)	SAT. FAT (gm)	CHOLES-TEROL (mg)	SODIUM (mg)	Exchanges
Chocolate Chip Cookies	1 (2.5 oz.)	330	41	4	17	7	5	170	3 starch, 2 fat
❦ Chocolate Cake	1 (3 oz.)	300	49	3	11	3	25	262	3 starch, 2 fat
❦ ⽇ Cheesecake	1 (3.5 oz.)	310	32	7	17	8	60	200	2 starch, 3 fat

NOT RECOMMENDED FOR USE

Products	SERVING SIZE	CALORIES	CARBO-HYDRATE (gm)	PROTEIN (gm)	FAT (gm)	SAT. FAT (gm)	CHOLES-TEROL (mg)	SODIUM (mg)	Exchanges
❦ ⽇ Danish (varieties)	1 (4 oz.)	520	75	7	16	4	0	230	
❦ ⽇ Cinnamon Rolls	1 (4 oz.)	460	70	7	18	1	0	230	
❦ ⚕ Fudge Moussecake	1 (4 oz.)	400	42	5	23	11	110	85	
❦ Shakes	Reg. Size	350	61	11	7	4	15	230	

⽇ = More than 2 fat exchanges per serving   ⚕ = More than 800 milligrams sodium   ❦ = High amounts of sugar

Products	SERVING SIZE	CALORIES	CARBO-HYDRATE (gm)	PROTEIN (gm)	FAT (gm)	SAT. FAT (gm)	CHOLES-TEROL (mg)	SODIUM (mg)	Exchanges

CHICK-FIL-A

Specialties

Products	SERVING SIZE	CALORIES	CARBO-HYDRATE (gm)	PROTEIN (gm)	FAT (gm)	SAT. FAT (gm)	CHOLES-TEROL (mg)	SODIUM (mg)	Exchanges
Chick-fil-A Chicken (no bun)	1 (3.6 oz.)	219	2	36	7	NA	42	552	5 lean meat
Chick-fil-A Sandwich (with bun)	1 (5.8 oz.)	360	28	41	9	NA	66	1174	2 starch, 5 lean meat
Chick-fil-A Deluxe Sandwich (with bun)	1 (7.5 oz.)	369	30	41	9	NA	66	1178	2 starch, 5 lean meat
Chick-fil-A Chargrilled Chicken (no bun)	1 (3.6 oz.)	128	1	26	3	NA	32	698	3½ lean meat
Chick-fil-A Chargrilled Sandwich (with bun)	1 (5.5 oz.)	258	24	30	5	NA	40	1121	1½ starch, 3½ lean meat
Chicken-fil-A Chargrilled Deluxe (with bun)	1 (7.2 oz.)	266	26	31	5	NA	40	1125	1½ starch 3½ lean meat
Chick-fil-A Grilled 'n Lites (2 skewers)	1 (2.7 oz.)	97	tr	20	2	NA	3	280	3 lean meat
Chick-fil-A Nuggets	8-pack (4 oz.)	287	13	28	15	NA	61	1326	1 starch, 3 lean meat, 1 fat
Chick-n-Q Sandwich	1 (6.8 oz.)	409	41	28	15	NA	10	1197	2½ starch, 3 lean meat, 1 fat
Chicken Salad Sandwich (on whole wheat)	1 (5.7 oz.)	365	26	24	18	NA	8	840	1½ starch, 3 lean meat, 2 fat
Hearty Breast of Chicken Soup	1 cup (8.5 oz.)	152	11	16	3	NA	46	722	1 starch, 2 lean meat
Chicken Salad Plate	1 (12.6 oz.)	291	10	22	19	NA	8	584	1 starch, 3 lean meat, 1 fat
Chargrilled Chicken Garden Salad	1 (10.4 oz.)	126	8	20	2	NA	28	567	1 vegetable, 2½ lean meat

Products	SERVING SIZE	CALORIES	CARBO-HYDRATE (gm)	PROTEIN (gm)	FAT (gm)	SAT. FAT (gm)	CHOLES-TEROL (mg)	SODIUM (mg)	Exchanges
Side Orders									
Tossed Salad	1 (4.5 oz.)	21	4	1	tr	NA	0	19	1 vegetable
⃝ with Ranch Dressing	1 (6 oz.)	298	6	1	30	NA	5	387	1 vegetable 6 fat
⃝ with Honey French Dressing	1 (6 oz.)	277	21	1	21	NA	0	396	1 vegetable, 1 starch, 4 fat
⃝ with Thousand Island Dressing	1 (6 oz.)	250	12	1	22	NA	25	396	1 vegetable, 5 fat
with Lite Italian Dressing	1 (6 oz.)	43	7	1	1	NA	0	856	1 vegetable
⃝ with Lite Ranch Dressing	1 (6 oz.)	171	8	2	15	NA	17	439	1 vegetable 3 fat
⃝ with Blue Cheese Dressing	1 (6 oz.)	243	6	3	24	NA	38	475	1 vegetable 5 fat
⃝ Cole Slaw	1 cup	175	11	1	14	NA	13	158	2 vegetable, 3 fat
⃝ Potato Salad	1 cup	198	14	3	15	NA	6	337	1 starch, 3 fat
Carrot-Raisin Salad	1 cup	116	18	1	5	NA	6	8	1 fruit, 1 vegetable, 1 fat
⃝ Waffle, Potato Fries	Small (3 oz.)	270	33	3	14	NA	8	45	2 starch, 3 fat
OCCASIONAL USE									
Icedream	Small cup (4.5 oz.)	134	19	4	5	NA	24	51	1 starch, 1 fat
♥ Lemon Pie	1 slice	329	64	8	5	NA	7	300	4 starch, 1 fat
⃝ ♥ Fudge Brownies w/Nuts	1 (2.8 oz.)	369	45	5	19	NA	31	213	3 starch, 3 fat
⃝ Cheesecake	1 slice	299	25	7	19	NA	13	272	1½ starch, 4 fat
⃝ ♥ with Strawberry Topping	(4.3 oz.)	343	35	7	19	NA	13	309	2 starch, 4 fat
⃝ ♥ with Blueberry Topping	(4.3 oz.)	350	37	7	19	NA	13	294	2 starch, 4 fat
♥ Lemonade	Small (10 fl. oz.)	138	34	tr	tr	NA	tr	tr	2 fruit

⃝ = More than 2 fat exchanges per serving   ⃝ = More than 800 milligrams sodium   ♥ = High amounts of sugar

Products	SERVING SIZE	CALORIES	CARBO-HYDRATE (gm)	PROTEIN (gm)	FAT (gm)	SAT. FAT (gm)	CHOLES-TEROL (mg)	SODIUM (mg)	Exchanges

CHURCH'S FRIED CHICKEN

Chicken

Products	SERVING SIZE	CALORIES	CARBO-HYDRATE (gm)	PROTEIN (gm)	FAT (gm)	SAT. FAT (gm)	CHOLES-TEROL (mg)	SODIUM (mg)	Exchanges
Fried Chicken Breast	1 (2.8 oz.)	200	4	19	12	NA	65	510	3 med. fat meat
Wing	1 (3.1 oz.)	250	8	19	16	NA	60	540	½ starch, 2 med. fat meat, 1 fat
Thigh	1 (2.8 oz.)	230	5	16	16	NA	80	520	2 med. fat meat, 1 fat
Leg	1 (2 oz.)	140	2	13	9	NA	45	160	2 med. fat meat

Accompaniments

Products	SERVING SIZE	CALORIES	CARBO-HYDRATE (gm)	PROTEIN (gm)	FAT (gm)	SAT. FAT (gm)	CHOLES-TEROL (mg)	SODIUM (mg)	Exchanges
Cajun Rice	3.1 oz.	130	16	1	7	NA	5	260	1 starch, 1 fat
Potatoes & Gravy	3.7 oz.	90	14	1	3	NA	0	520	1 starch
Corn on the Cob	5.7 oz.	190	32	8	5	NA	0	15	2 starch, 1 fat
French Fries	2.7 oz.	210	29	3	11	NA	0	605	2 starch, 2 fat
Okra	2.8 oz.	210	19	3	16	NA	0	520	1 starch, 3 fat
Biscuits	2.1 oz.	250	26	2	16	NA	5	640	2 starch, 2 fat
Cole Slaw	3 oz.	92	8	4	6	NA	0	230	1 vegetable, 1 fat

OCCASIONAL USE

Products	SERVING SIZE	CALORIES	CARBO-HYDRATE (gm)	PROTEIN (gm)	FAT (gm)	SAT. FAT (gm)	CHOLES-TEROL (mg)	SODIUM (mg)	Exchanges
Apple Pie	3.1 oz.	280	41	2	12	NA	5	340	2 starch, 1 fruit 2 fat

COLOMBO

Products	SERVING SIZE	CALORIES	CARBO-HYDRATE (gm)	PROTEIN (gm)	FAT (gm)	SAT. FAT (gm)	CHOLES-TEROL (mg)	SODIUM (mg)	Exchanges
Lowfat Frozen Yogurt	½ cup	99	18	3	2	NA	10	35	1 starch, ½ fat
Lite Nonfat Frozen Yogurt	½ cup	95	21	4	0	NA	0	70	1½ starch

DAIRY QUEEN

Sandwiches

Products	SERVING SIZE	CALORIES	CARBO-HYDRATE (gm)	PROTEIN (gm)	FAT (gm)	SAT. FAT (gm)	CHOLES-TEROL (mg)	SODIUM (mg)	Exchanges
Single Hamburger	1 (5 oz.)	310	29	17	13	6	45	580	2 starch, 2 med. fat meat

Products	SERVING SIZE	CALORIES	CARBO- HYDRATE (gm)	PROTEIN (gm)	FAT (gm)	SAT. FAT (gm)	CHOLES- TEROL (mg)	SODIUM (mg)	Exchanges
Double Hamburger	1 (7 oz.)	460	29	31	25	12	95	630	2 starch, 4 med. fat meat
Single w/Cheese	1 (5.5 oz.)	365	30	20	18	9	60	800	2 starch, 2 med. fat meat, 1 fat
☀ Double w/Cheese	1 (8 oz.)	570	31	37	34	18	120	1070	2 starch, 4½ med. fat meat, 2 fat
☷ ☀ DQ Homestyle Ultimate Burger	1 (9.7 oz.)	700	30	43	47	21	140	1110	2 starch, 5 med. fat meat, 4 fat
Hot Dog	1 (3.5 oz.)	280	23	9	16	6	25	700	1½ starch, 1 med. fat meat, 2 fat
☷ Hot Dog w/Chili	1 (4.5 oz.)	320	26	11	19	7	30	720	1½ starch, 1 med. fat meat, 3 fat
☷ ☀ Hot Dog w/Cheese	1 (4 oz.)	330	24	12	21	9	55	920	1½ starch, 1 med. fat meat, 3 fat
☷ ☀ Quarter Pound Super Dog	1 (7 oz.)	590	41	20	38	16	60	1360	3 starch, 2 med. fat meat, 5 fat
BBQ Beef Sandwich	1 (4.5 oz.)	225	34	12	4	1	20	700	2 starch, 1 med. fat meat
Fish Fillet Sandwich	1 (6 oz.)	370	39	16	16	3	45	630	2½ starch, 1 med. fat meat, 2 fat
☀ Fish Fillet w/Cheese	1 (6.5 oz.)	420	40	19	21	7	60	850	2½ starch, 2 med. fat meat, 2 fat
Grilled Chicken Fillet Sandwich	1 (6.5 oz.)	300	33	25	8	2	50	800	2 starch, 3 lean meat
Breaded Chicken Fillet Sandwich	1 (6.7 oz.)	430	37	24	20	4	55	760	2½ starch, 2½ med. fat meat, 1 fat
☀ Breaded Chicken Fillet w/Cheese	1 (7.2 oz.)	480	38	27	25	7	70	980	2½ starch, 3 med. fat meat, 2 fat

Side Orders

Products	SERVING SIZE	CALORIES	CARBO- HYDRATE (gm)	PROTEIN (gm)	FAT (gm)	SAT. FAT (gm)	CHOLES- TEROL (mg)	SODIUM (mg)	Exchanges
French Fries	Small	210	29	3	10	2	0	115	1½ starch, 2 fat
French Fries	Regular	300	40	4	14	3	0	160	2½ starch, 2½ fat
☷ French Fries	Large	390	52	5	18	4	0	200	3½ starch, 3 fat
Onion Rings	1 (3 oz.)	240	29	4	12	3	0	135	2 starch, 2 fat
Side Salad without Dressing	1 (4.8 oz.)	25	4	1	0	0	0	15	1 vegetable

☷ = More than 2 fat exchanges per serving   ☀ = More than 800 milligrams sodium   ✿ = High amounts of sugar

Products	SERVING SIZE	CALORIES	CARBO-HYDRATE (gm)	PROTEIN (gm)	FAT (gm)	SAT. FAT (gm)	CHOLES-TEROL (mg)	SODIUM (mg)	Exchanges
Garden Salad without Dressing	1 (10 oz.)	200	7	13	13	7	185	240	1 vegetable, 2 med. fat meat, 1 fat
Thousand Island Dressing	2 oz.	225	10	tr	21	3	25	570	½ starch, 4 fat
Reduced Calorie French Dressing	2 oz.	90	11	tr	5	1	0	450	½ starch, 1 fat
Lettuce	.5 oz.	2	0	0	0	0	0	1	Free
Tomato	.5 oz.	3	0	0	0	0	0	1	Free

OCCASIONAL USE

Products	SERVING SIZE	CALORIES	CARBO-HYDRATE (gm)	PROTEIN (gm)	FAT (gm)	SAT. FAT (gm)	CHOLES-TEROL (mg)	SODIUM (mg)	Exchanges
Vanilla Cone	Small	140	22	4	4	3	15	60	1½ starch, 1 fat
Vanilla Cone	Regular	230	36	6	7	5	20	95	2½ starch, 1 fat
Vanilla Cone	Large	340	53	8	10	7	30	140	3½ starch, 1½ fat
Chocolate Cone	Regular	230	36	6	7	5	20	115	2½ fat, 1 fat
Chocolate Cone	Large	350	54	8	11	8	30	170	3½ starch, 1½ fat
Chocolate Dipped Cone	Regular	330	40	6	16	8	20	100	2½ starch, 3 fat
Chocolate Sundae	Regular	300	54	6	7	5	20	140	3½ starch, 1 fat
Strawberry Waffle Cone Sundae	1 (6 oz.)	350	56	8	12	5	20	220	3½ starch, 2 fat
DQ Sandwich	1 (2 oz.)	140	24	3	4	2	5	135	1½ starch, 1 fat
Dilly Bar	1 (3 oz.)	210	21	3	13	6	10	50	1½ starch, 2 fat
Mr. Misty	Regular	250	63	0	0	0	0	0	4 fruit
Yogurt Cone	Regular	180	38	6	tr	tr	tr	80	2½ starch
Yogurt Cone	Large	260	56	9	tr	tr	5	115	3½ starch
Cup of Yogurt	Regular	170	35	6	tr	tr	tr	70	2 starch
Cup of Yogurt	Large	230	49	8	tr	tr	tr	100	3 starch
Yogurt Strawberry Sundae	Regular	200	43	6	tr	tr	tr	80	2 starch, 1 fruit
Strawberry Breeze	Small	290	63	9	tr	tr	5	115	4 starch
QC Vanilla Big Scoop	1 (4.5 oz.)	300	39	5	14	9	35	100	2½ starch, 2½ fat
QC Chocolate Big Scoope	1 (4.5 oz.)	310	40	5	14	10	35	100	2½ starch, 2½ fat

Products	SERVING SIZE	CALORIES	CARBO-HYDRATE (gm)	PROTEIN (gm)	FAT (gm)	SAT. FAT (gm)	CHOLES-TEROL (mg)	SODIUM (mg)	Exchanges
NOT RECOMMENDED FOR USE									
Vanilla Shake	Regular	520	88	12	14	8	45	230	
Vanilla Shake	Large	600	101	13	16	10	50	260	
Chocolate Shake	Regular	540	94	12	14	8	45	290	
Vanilla Malt	Regular	610	106	13	14	8	45	230	
Banana Split	1 (13 oz.)	510	93	9	11	8	30	250	
Peanut Buster Parfait	1 10.8 oz.)	710	94	16	32	10	30	410	
Hot Fudge Brownie Delight	1 (10.8 oz.)	710	102	11	29	14	35	340	
Nutty Double Fudge	(9.7 oz.)	580	85	10	22	10	35	170	
Buster Bar	1 5.25 oz.)	450	40	11	29	9	15	220	
Strawberry Blizzard	Small	400	64	9	12	8	35	160	
Strawberry Blizzard	Regular	570	92	13	16	11	50	230	
Heath Blizzard	Small	560	79	11	23	11	40	280	
Heath Blizzard	Regular	820	114	16	36	17	60	410	
DQ Frozen Cake	1 (5.8 oz.)	380	50	6	18	8	20	210	
Strawberry Breeze	Regular	420	90	12	1	tr	5	170	
Heath Breeze	Small	450	78	11	12	3	10	230	
Heath Breeze	Regular	680	113	15	21	6	15	360	

目 = More than 2 fat exchanges per serving   ♦ = More than 800 milligrams sodium   ♠ = High amounts of sugar

Products	SERVING SIZE	CALORIES	CARBO-HYDRATE (gm)	PROTEIN (gm)	FAT (gm)	SAT. FAT (gm)	CHOLES-TEROL (mg)	SODIUM (mg)	Exchanges

DENNY'S

Sandwiches

Products	SERVING SIZE	CALORIES	CARBO-HYDRATE (gm)	PROTEIN (gm)	FAT (gm)	SAT. FAT (gm)	CHOLES-TEROL (mg)	SODIUM (mg)	Exchanges
DennyBurger	1	629	37	35	37	NA	NA	427	3½ starch, 4 med. fat meat, 2 fat
Club Sandwich	1	590	41	36	20	NA	NA	582	3 starch, 4 med. fat meat
Grilled Cheese	1	454	29	17	29	NA	NA	1519	2 starch, 2 med. fat meat, 3 fat
Grilled Chicken	1	439	40	27	12	NA	NA	413	2½ starch, 3 med. fat meat
Superbird	1	625	81	37	24	NA	NA	1750	5 starch, 3 med. fat meat
Veggie Cheese	1	350	29	21	20	NA	NA	909	2 starch, 2 med. fat meat, 1 fat
Patty Melt	1	761	27	40	47	NA	NA	887	2 starch, 5 med. fat meat, 4 fat
BLT	1	492	42	17	34	NA	NA	662	3 starch, 1 med. fat meat, 4 fat
Works Burger	1	944	48	49	61	NA	NA	1306	3 starch, 6 med. fat meat, 6 fat
Bacon-Swiss	1	819	38	53	52	NA	NA	1127	2½ starch, 7 med. fat meat, 2 fat
San Fran Burger	1	872	51	58	48	NA	NA	1335	3 starch, 7 med. fat meat, 3 fat
Senior Turkey Sandwich	1	340	26	24	27	3	75	1000	2 starch, 3 med. fat meat, 1 fat

Salads

Products	SERVING SIZE	CALORIES	CARBO-HYDRATE (gm)	PROTEIN (gm)	FAT (gm)	SAT. FAT (gm)	CHOLES-TEROL (mg)	SODIUM (mg)	Exchanges
California Chicken Salad	1	325	7	28	15	NA	NA	460	1 vegetable, 4 lean meat, 1 fat
Chef's Salad	1	492	13	36	20	NA	NA	1370	2 vegetable, 5 med. fat meat
Garden Salad	1	38	4	5	3	NA	NA	30	1 vegetable
Tuna Salad	1	340	13	30	18	NA	NA	652	1 starch, 4 med. fat meat
Cole Slaw	1 cup	119	8	1	10	NA	NA	149	1 vegetable, 2 fat

Products	SERVING SIZE	CALORIES	CARBO-HYDRATE (gm)	PROTEIN (gm)	FAT (gm)	SAT. FAT (gm)	CHOLES-TEROL (mg)	SODIUM (mg)	Exchanges
🛢☂ Taco Salad with Fried Tortilla Shell	1	953	72	37	50	NA	NA	2628	5 starch, 4 med. fat meat, 6 fat
Guacamole	1 oz.	60	2	1	6	NA	NA	130	1 fat
Ranch Dressing	1 Tbsp.	52	tr	tr	6	NA	NA	117	1 fat
Soup/Chili									
🛢☂ Clam Chowder	1 bowl	235	21	5	14	NA	NA	856	1½ starch, 3 fat
☂ Split Pea Soup	1 bowl	231	33	14	5	NA	NA	1519	2 starch, I med. fat meat
🛢☂ Cheese Soup	1 bowl	309	19	5	22	NA	NA	898	1 starch, 5 fat
☂ Chicken Noodle	1 bowl	105	15	4	3	NA	NA	1118	1 starch, ½ fat
☂ Beef Barley	1 bowl	79	11	5	2	NA	NA	847	1 starch
Potato Soup	1 bowl	241	31	3	13	NA	NA	772	2 starch, 2 fat
☂ Chili	8 oz.	338	30	19	15	NA	NA	1354	2 starch, 2 med. fat meat, 1 fat
Dinner Entrees									
Chicken-Fried Steak	1 order	252	16	14	15	NA	NA	422	1 starch, 2 med. fat meat, 1 fat
Grilled Chicken	1 order	206	tr	40	5	NA	NA	420	5 lean meat
Halibut Steak	1 order	185	tr	35	4	NA	NA	92	4 lean meat
🛢 Catfish	2-4 oz.	576	0	32	48	NA	NA	460	4½ med. fat meat, 5 fat
Stir-Fry	1 order	328	5	36	11	NA	NA	109	5 lean meat
Top Sirloin Steak	1 order	223	tr	36	7	NA	NA	62	5 lean meat
New York Steak	1 order	582	0	65	36	NA	NA	100	9 lean meat, 2 fat
Shrimp, Fried	5 shrimp	230	37	15	2	NA	NA	393	2½ starch, 1 lean meat
Liver with Bacon & Onions	2 slices	334	10	40	15	NA	NA	516	1 vegetable, 7 lean meat
☂ Fried Chicken	4 pieces	463	8	62	30	NA	NA	1304	½ starch, 8 lean meat

🛢 = More than 2 fat exchanges per serving   ☂ = More than 800 milligrams sodium   ✿ = High amounts of sugar

Products	SERVING SIZE	CALORIES	CARBO-HYDRATE (gm)	PROTEIN (gm)	FAT (gm)	SAT. FAT (gm)	CHOLES-TEROL (mg)	SODIUM (mg)	Exchanges
⍓ Turkey with Stuffing	6 slices	505	40	56	14	NA	NA	895	3 starch, 7 lean meat
⍓ Roast Beef Dinner	1	965	41	60	32	6	180	820	3 starch, 7 med. fat meat
⍟ Spaghetti & Meatballs	1	1000	119	37	38	NA	110	170	8 starch, 3 med. fat meat, 3 fat

Accompaniments

Baked Potato	1	90	21	3	0	NA	NA	7	1½ starch
⍟ French Fries	1 order	303	38	2	16	NA	NA	74	2½ starch, 3 fat
Mashed Potatoes	1 order	74	15	2	tr	NA	NA	302	1 starch
Rice Pilaf	1 order	89	15	2	2	NA	NA	320	1 starch
Peas	3 oz.	40	7	3	tr	NA	NA	54	1 vegetable
Carrots	3 oz.	17	4	tr	tr	NA	NA	31	1 vegetable
Corn	3 oz.	63	15	2	tr	NA	NA	37	1 starch
Green Beans	3 oz.	13	3	1	tr	NA	NA	22	1 vegetable
Onion Rings	2 rings	172	18	2	10	NA	NA	396	1 starch, 2 fat

Breakfast Items

Pancakes	1	136	26	4	2	NA	NA	656	2 starch
Biscuit	1	217	35	4	7	NA	NA	800	2 starch, 1 fat
Country Gravy	1 oz.	140	14	8	8	NA	NA	712	1 starch, 1 fat
Waffle	1	261	35	6	10	NA	NA	62	2 starch, 2 fat
Hashed Browns	4 oz.	164	32	4	2	NA	NA	310	2 starch
⍓ Ham Slice	1	156	tr	14	7	NA	NA	1303	2 lean meat
Blueberry Muffin	1	309	42	4	14	NA	NA	190	3 starch, 2 fat
Cinnamon Roll	1	450	73	9	14	NA	NA	750	5 starch, 2 fat
Sausage	1 link	113	0	3	10	NA	NA	250	2 fat
Bacon	1 slice	48	tr	3	4	NA	NA	142	1 fat
Bagel	1	240	47	9	1	NA	NA	450	3 starch
⍟ French Toast	2 slices	729	46	12	56	NA	NA	275	3 starch, 1 med. fat meat, 9 fat
⍓ Eggs Benedict	1 order	658	20	33	36	NA	NA	2197	1 starch, 5 med. fat meat, 2 fat

Products	SERVING SIZE	CALORIES	CARBO-HYDRATE (gm)	PROTEIN (gm)	FAT (gm)	SAT. FAT (gm)	CHOLES-TEROL (mg)	SODIUM (mg)	Exchanges
ᗟ Ultimate Omelette	1 order	577	8	25	41	NA	NA	649	4 med. fat meat, 4 fat
Denver Omelette	1 order	567	11	47	27	NA	NA	507	2 vegetable, 6 med. fat meat
☀ Chili Cheese Omelette	1 order	490	17	28	32	2	230	1130	1 starch, 4 med. fat fat meat, 2 fat
☀ Ham 'N Cheddar	1 order	480	7	28	33	2	235	1120	½ starch, 4 high fat meat, 1 fat
ᗟ ☀ Mexican Omelette	1 order	540	14	29	40	6	245	1060	1 starch, 4 med. fat meat, 4 fat

DOMINO'S PIZZA

Pizza

Products	SERVING SIZE	CALORIES	CARBO-HYDRATE (gm)	PROTEIN (gm)	FAT (gm)	SAT. FAT (gm)	CHOLES-TEROL (mg)	SODIUM (mg)	Exchanges
Cheese Pizza 16" (large)	2 slices (5.5 oz.)	376	56	22	10	6	19	483	4 starch, 2 med. fat meat
☀ Pepperoni Pizza 16" (large)	2 slices (5.5 oz.)	460	56	24	18	9	28	825	4 starch, 2 med. fat meat, 2 fat
Sausage/Mushroom Pizza 16" (large)	2 slices (5.5 oz.)	430	55	24	16	8	28	552	4 starch, 2 med. fat meat, 1 fat
☀ Veggie Pizza 16" (large) includes mushrooms, onion, green pepper, double cheese, olives	2 slices (5.5 oz.)	498	60	31	19	10	36	1035	4 starch, 3 med. fat meat, 1 fat
☀ Deluxe Pizza 16" (large) includes sausage, pepperoni, onion, green pepper, mushrooms	2 slices (5.5 oz.)	498	59	27	20	9	40	954	4 starch, 2 med. fat meat, 2 fat
☀ Double Cheese/ Pepperoni Pizza 16" (large)	2 slices (5.5 oz.)	545	55	32	25	13	48	1042	4 starch, 3 med. fat meat, 2 fat
☀ Ham Pizza 16" (large)	2 slices (5.5 oz.)	417	58	23	11	6	26	805	4 starch, 2 med. fat meat

Products	SERVING SIZE	CALORIES	CARBO-HYDRATE (gm)	PROTEIN (gm)	FAT (gm)	SAT. FAT (gm)	CHOLES-TEROL (mg)	SODIUM (mg)	Exchanges

GODFATHER'S PIZZA

Original Crust

Products	SERVING SIZE	CALORIES	CARBO-HYDRATE (gm)	PROTEIN (gm)	FAT (gm)	SAT. FAT (gm)	CHOLES-TEROL (mg)	SODIUM (mg)	Exchanges
Cheese Pizza mini	¼ of whole (2 oz.)	138	20	6	4	NA	13	159	1½ starch, 1 fat
Cheese Pizza small	⅙ of whole (3.5 oz.)	239	32	10	7	NA	25	289	2 starch, 1 med. fat meat
Cheese Pizza medium	⅛ of whole (3.6 oz.)	242	35	10	7	NA	22	285	2 starch, 1 med. fat meat
Cheese Pizza large	⅒ of whole (4 oz.)	271	37	12	8	NA	28	329	2½ starch, 1 med. fat meat
Combo Pizza mini	¼ of whole (2.8 oz.)	164	21	8	5	NA	17	287	1½ starch, 1 med. fat meat
Combo Pizza small	⅙ of whole (5 oz.)	299	34	15	11	NA	37	573	2 starch, 2 med. fat meat
Combo Pizza medium	⅛ of whole (5.2 oz.)	318	37	16	12	NA	38	569	2½ starch, 2 med. fat meat
Combo Pizza large	⅒ of whole (5.6 oz.)	332	39	16	12	NA	39	617	2½ starch, 2 med. fat meat

Golden Crust

Products	SERVING SIZE	CALORIES	CARBO-HYDRATE (gm)	PROTEIN (gm)	FAT (gm)	SAT. FAT (gm)	CHOLES-TEROL (mg)	SODIUM (mg)	Exchanges
Cheese Pizza small	⅙ of whole (3 oz.)	213	27	8	8	NA	19	258	2 starch, 1 med. fat meat
Cheese Pizza medium	⅛ of whole (3 oz.)	229	28	8	9	NA	19	272	2 starch, 1 med. fat meat
Cheese Pizza large	⅒ of whole (3.6 oz.)	261	31	8	11	NA	23	314	2 starch, 1 med. fat meat, 1 fat
Combo Pizza small	⅙ of whole (4.5 oz.)	273	29	13	12	NA	31	542	2 starch, 1 med. fat meat, 1 fat

Products	SERVING SIZE	CALORIES	CARBO-HYDRATE (gm)	PROTEIN (gm)	FAT (gm)	SAT. FAT (gm)	CHOLES-TEROL (mg)	SODIUM (mg)	Exchanges
Combo Pizza medium	1/8 of whole (4.5 oz.)	283	30	13	13	NA	29	526	2 starch, 1 med. fat meat, 1 fat
Combo Pizza large	1/10 of whole (5.1 oz.)	322	33	14	15	NA	34	602	2 starch, 1 med. fat meat, 2 fat

GOLDEN CORRAL

Entrees

Products	SERVING SIZE	CALORIES	CARBO-HYDRATE (gm)	PROTEIN (gm)	FAT (gm)	SAT. FAT (gm)	CHOLES-TEROL (mg)	SODIUM (mg)	Exchanges
Sirloin	5-oz.	230	0	27	14	NA	85	270	4 lean meat
Ribeye	Regular (5 oz.)	450	0	34	35	NA	120	220	5 med fat meat, 2 fat
Sirloin Tips w/Onions & Peppers	1 order (8 oz.)	290	8	30	13	NA	120	260	1 vegetable, 4 lean meat
Chopped Sirloin	Regular (4 oz.)	320	0	28	23	NA	100	160	4 med fat meat, 1 fat
Golden Grilled Chicken	1 order (4 oz.)	170	0	32	5	NA	100	520	4 lean meat
Golden Fried Chicken Fillets	1 order (5.5 oz.)	370	14	37	19	NA	85	570	1 starch, 5 med. fat meat
Golden Fried Shrimp	1 order (3 oz.)	250	24	12	12	NA	90	470	1½ starch, 1 med. fat meat, 1 fat

Side Orders

Products	SERVING SIZE	CALORIES	CARBO-HYDRATE (gm)	PROTEIN (gm)	FAT (gm)	SAT. FAT (gm)	CHOLES-TEROL (mg)	SODIUM (mg)	Exchanges
Baked Potato	1 (7.7 oz.)	220	46	5	2	NA	0	60	3 starch
Texas Toast	1 order (1.7 oz.)	170	26	5	6	NA	0	230	2 starch, 1 fat

HARDEE'S

Sandwiches/Subs

Products	SERVING SIZE	CALORIES	CARBO-HYDRATE (gm)	PROTEIN (gm)	FAT (gm)	SAT. FAT (gm)	CHOLES-TEROL (mg)	SODIUM (mg)	Exchanges
Hamburger	1 (3.5 oz.)	260	33	10	10	4	30	510	2 starch, 1 med. fat meat, 1 fat
Cheeseburger	1 (4.3 oz.)	300	34	12	14	6	40	740	2 starch, 1 med. fat meat, 2 fat

目 = More than 2 fat exchanges per serving   ⌿ = More than 800 milligrams sodium   ♥ = High amounts of sugar

Products	SERVING SIZE	CALORIES	CARBO-HYDRATE (gm)	PROTEIN (gm)	FAT (gm)	SAT. FAT (gm)	CHOLES-TEROL (mg)	SODIUM (mg)	Exchanges
Quarter-Pound Cheeseburger	1 (6.4 oz.)	500	34	29	29	14	70	1060	2 starch, 3 med. fat meat, 3 fat
Big Deluxe Burger	1 (7.6 oz.)	500	32	27	30	12	70	760	2 starch, 3 med. fat meat, 3 fat
Bacon Cheeseburger	1 (7.7 oz.)	610	31	34	39	16	80	1030	2 starch, 4 med. fat meat, 3 fat
Mushroom N Swiss Burger	1 (6.5 oz.)	490	33	30	27	13	70	940	2 starch, 3½ med. fat meat, 2 fat
Frisco Burger	1 (8.5 oz.)	760	43	36	50	18	70	1280	3 starch, 4 med. fat meat, 5 fat
Real West Bacon & Cheese Burger	1 (7.6 oz.)	560	38	33	31	14	45	1130	2½ starch, 3½ med. fat meat, 2½ fat
New York Patty Melt	1 (8.5 oz.)	780	45	35	51	20	80	990	3 starch, 3½ med. fat meat, 6 fat
Roast Beef Sandwich	Regular (4 oz.)	280	29	18	11	4	40	870	2 starch, 2 med. fat meat
Big Roast Beef Sandwich	1 (4.7 oz.)	380	29	26	18	8	60	1230	2 starch, 3 med. fat meat
Real West BBQ Beef Sandwich	1 (7 oz.)	350	48	18	9	4	36	1290	3 starch, 1 med. fat meat, 1 fat
Hot Ham N Cheese	1 (5.25 oz.)	330	32	23	12	5	65	1420	2 starch, 2½ med. fat meat
Fisherman's Fillet	1 (7.5 oz.)	480	50	23	21	6	70	1210	3 starch, 2 med. fat meat, 2 fat
Turkey Club	1 (7.3 oz.)	390	32	29	16	4	70	1280	2 starch, 3 med. fat meat
Frisco Club	1 (8.5 oz.)	620	46	30	35	11	75	1930	3 starch, 3 med. fat meat, 4 fat
Chicken Fillet	1 (6 oz.)	370	44	19	13	2	55	1060	3 starch, 2 med. fat meat
Frisco Chicken	1 (8.6 oz.)	620	44	35	34	10	95	1730	3 starch, 3½ med. fat meat, 3 fat
Grilled Chicken Breast Sandwich	1 (6.8 oz.)	310	34	24	9	1	60	890	2 starch, 2½ lean meat
Big Twin	1 (6 oz.)	450	34	23	25	11	55	580	2 starch, 3 med. fat meat, 2 fat

	Products	SERVING SIZE	CALORIES	CARBO-HYDRATE (gm)	PROTEIN (gm)	FAT (gm)	SAT. FAT (gm)	CHOLES-TEROL (mg)	SODIUM (mg)	Exchanges
†	Reuben Sandwich	1 (9.3 oz.)	540	48	35	22	6	80	1610	3 starch, 4 med. fat meat
	Hot Dog	1 (4 oz.)	290	26	11	16	4	30	760	2 starch, 1 high fat meat, 1 fat
†	Turkey Sub	1 (9.3 oz.)	390	53	29	7	4	65	1420	3½ starch, 2½ lean meat
†	Roast Beef Sub	1 (9 oz.)	370	57	23	5	3	45	1400	3½ starch, 2 lean meat
†	Ham Sub	1 (8.6 oz.)	370	52	25	7	4	45	1400	3½ starch, 2 lean meat
†	Combo Sub	1 (9 oz.)	380	52	28	6	3	45	1440	3½ starch 2½ lean meat
	Fried Chicken Breast	1 (4 oz.)	340	15	27	19	7	104	659	1 starch, 3 med. fat meat, 1 fat
	Wing	(2 oz.)	205	9	12	13	5	48	374	½ starch, 1½ med. fat meat, 1 fat
	Thigh	1 (3.8 oz.)	370	13	20	26	9	128	489	1 starch, 2½ med. fat meat, 2 fat
	Leg	1 (2 oz.)	152	6	12	8	3	80	207	½ starch, 1½ med. fat meat
	Chicken Stix	6 Pieces (3.5 oz.)	210	13	19	9	2	35	680	1 starch, 2 med. fat meat
†	Chicken Stix	9 Pieces (5.3 oz.)	310	20	28	14	3	55	1020	1 starch, 3 med. fat meat
	Side Orders									
	Garden Salad without Dressing	1 (7.8 oz.)	184	3	12	12	7	34	250	1 vegetable, 1½ med. fat meat, 1 fat
	Side Salad without Dressing	1 (4 oz.)	20	1	2	tr	tr	0	15	Free
†	Chef Salad without Dressing	1 (9.5 oz.)	214	5	20	13	8	44	910	1 vegetable, 2½ med. fat meat
▮	Cole Slaw	4 oz.	240	13	2	20	3	10	340	2 vegetables, 4 fat
▮ †	Cole Slaw	12 oz.	710	38	5	60	10	35	1020	2 vegetables, 1½ starch, 12 fat

▮ = More than 2 fat exchanges per serving † = More than 800 milligrams sodium ♥ = High amounts of sugar

Products	SERVING SIZE	CALORIES	CARBO-HYDRATE (gm)	PROTEIN (gm)	FAT (gm)	SAT. FAT (gm)	CHOLES-TEROL (mg)	SODIUM (mg)	Exchanges
French Fries	Regular (2.5 oz.)	230	30	3	11	2	0	85	2 starch, 2 fat
French Fries	Large (4 oz.)	360	48	4	17	3	0	135	3 starch, 3 fat
Big Fry	1 (5.5 oz.)	500	66	6	23	5	0	180	4 starch, 4 fat
Crispy Curls	1 (3 oz.)	300	36	4	16	3	0	840	2 starch, 3 fat
Mashed Potatoes	1 (4 oz.)	70	16	2	tr	tr	0	260	1 starch
Mashed Potatoes	1 (12 oz.)	220	48	6	tr	tr	0	760	3 starch
Gravy	1 (1.5 oz.)	20	3	1	tr	tr	0	260	Free
Gravy	1 (5 oz.)	60	11	3	1	tr	5	850	1 starch

Breakfast Items

Products	SERVING SIZE	CALORIES	CARBO-HYDRATE (gm)	PROTEIN (gm)	FAT (gm)	SAT. FAT (gm)	CHOLES-TEROL (mg)	SODIUM (mg)	Exchanges
Rise N Shine Biscuit	1 (3 oz.)	320	34	5	18	3	0	740	2 starch, 4 fat
Cinnamon 'N Raisin Biscuit	1 (3 oz.)	320	37	4	17	5	0	510	2½ starch 3 fat
Sausage Biscuit	1 (4 oz.)	440	34	13	28	7	25	1100	2 starch, 1 high fat meat, 4 fat
Sausage & Egg Biscuit	1 (5.3 oz.)	490	35	18	31	8	170	1150	2 starch, 2 med. fat meat, 4 fat
Bacon Biscuit	1 (3.2 oz.)	360	34	10	21	4	10	950	2 starch, 4 fat
Bacon & Egg Biscuit	1 (4.4 oz.)	410	35	15	24	5	155	990	2 starch, 1 med. fat meat, 4 fat
Bacon, Egg, Cheese Biscuit	1 (4.8 oz.)	460	35	17	28	8	165	1220	2 starch, 2 med. fat meat, 4 fat
Steak Biscuit	1 (5 oz.)	500	46	15	29	7	30	1320	3 starch, 1 med. fat meat, 4 fat
Steak, Egg Biscuit	1 (6.3 oz.)	550	47	20	32	8	175	1370	3 starch, 2 med. fat meat, 4 fat
Chicken Biscuit	1 (5 oz.)	430	42	17	22	4	45	1330	3 starch, 2 med. fat meat, 1 fat
Ham Biscuit	1 (3.7 oz.)	320	34	10	16	2	15	1000	2 starch, 1 med. fat meat, 2 fat
Ham, Egg Biscuit	1 (4.9 oz.)	370	35	15	19	4	160	1050	2 starch, 1½ med. fat meat, 2 fat

Products	SERVING SIZE	CALORIES	CARBO-HYDRATE (gm)	PROTEIN (gm)	FAT (gm)	SAT. FAT (gm)	CHOLES-TEROL (mg)	SODIUM (mg)	Exchanges
Ham, Egg, Cheese Biscuit	1 (5.3 oz.)	420	35	18	23	6	170	1270	2 starch, 2 med. fat meat, 3 fat
Country Ham Biscuit	1 (3.8 oz.)	350	35	11	18	3	25	1550	2 starch, 1 med. fat meat, 3 fat
Country Ham, Egg Biscuit	1 (4.9 oz.)	400	35	16	22	4	175	1600	2 starch, 1½ med. fat meat, 3 fat
Canadian Rise N Shine Biscuit	1 (5.7 oz.)	470	35	22	27	8	180	1550	2 starch, 2 med. fat meat, 4 fat
Big Country Breakfast Bacon	1 (7.6 oz.)	660	51	24	40	10	305	1540	3½ starch, 2 med. fat meat, 5 fat
Big Country Breakfast Ham	1(8.8 oz.)	620	51	28	33	7	325	1780	3½ starch, 2½ med. fat meat, 4 fat
Big Country Breakfast Sausage	1 (10 oz.)	850	51	33	57	16	340	1980	3½ starch, 3 med. fat meat, 8 fat
Big Country Breakfast Country Ham	1 (9 oz.)	670	52	29	38	9	345	2870	3½ starch, 2½ med. fat meat, 5 fat
Ultimate Omelet Biscuit	1 (5.3 oz.)	540	36	16	36	12	80	1120	2½ starch, 1 med. fat meat, 6 fat
Frisco Sausage Breakfast Sandwich	1 (8 oz.)	720	43	33	47	17	205	1740	3 starch, 3 med. fat meat, 6 fat
Frisco Ham Breakfast Sandwich	1 (6.5 oz.)	460	46	20	22	8	175	1320	3 starch, 2 med. fat meat, 2 fat
Strawberry Cream Cheese Strudel	1 (3.5 oz.)	320	34	5	19	5	5	260	1 starch, 1 fruit 4 fat
Hash Rounds Potatoes	1 (2.8 oz.)	230	24	3	14	3	0	560	1½ starch, 3 fat
Biscuit 'N Gravy	1 (8 oz.)	440	45	9	24	6	15	1250	3 starch, 5 fat
Pancakes	3 (4.8 oz.)	280	56	8	2	1	15	890	3½ starch
Pancakes with Sausage Pattie	3 (4.8 oz.) 1 (1.4 oz.)	430	56	16	16	6	40	1290	3½ starch 1 med. fat meat, 2 fat
Pancakes with Bacon Strips	3 (4.8 oz.) 2 (.5 oz.)	350	56	13	9	3	25	1110	3½ starch 2 fat
Blueberry Muffin	1 (4 oz.)	400	56	7	17	4	65	310	3½ starch, 3 fat

B = More than 2 fat exchanges per serving   ☀ = More than 800 milligrams sodium   ❀ = High amounts of sugar

Products	SERVING SIZE	CALORIES	CARBO-HYDRATE (gm)	PROTEIN (gm)	FAT (gm)	SAT. FAT (gm)	CHOLES-TEROL (mg)	SODIUM (mg)	Exchanges
Oatbran Raisin Muffin	1 (4.3 oz.)	410	59	8	16	3	50	380	4 starch 2 fat
Orange Juice	11 oz.	140	34	2	tr	tr	0	5	2 fruit

OCCASIONAL USE

Products	SERVING SIZE	CALORIES	CARBO-HYDRATE (gm)	PROTEIN (gm)	FAT (gm)	SAT. FAT (gm)	CHOLES-TEROL (mg)	SODIUM (mg)	Exchanges
❦ Apple Turnover	1 (3.2 oz.)	270	38	3	12	4	0	250	2½ starch, 2 fat
❦ Big Cookie	1 (1.7 oz.)	250	31	3	13	4	5	240	2 starch, 2 fat
❦ Cool Twist Cone Chocolate	1 (4 oz.)	180	29	4	4	3	15	85	2 starch, 1 fat
❦ Cool Twist Cone Vanilla	1 (4 oz.)	180	29	5	4	3	15	80	2 starch, 1 fat
❦ Cool Twist Cone Vanilla/Chocolate	1 (4 oz.)	170	29	5	4	3	15	85	2 starch, 1 fat
❦ Vanilla Shake	1 (11.5 oz.)	370	59	14	9	6	25	210	4 starch, 2 fat
❦ Chocolate Shake	1 (11.5 oz.)	390	61	15	10	6	31	220	4 starch, 2 fat
❦ Strawberry Shake	1 (12 oz.)	390	65	13	8	5	30	200	4 starch, 2 fat
❦ Butterfinger Shake	1 (12 oz.)	370	55	12	9	6	32	180	4 starch, 2 fat
❦ Cool Twist Sundae Hot Fudge	1 (6 oz.)	320	50	8	10	5	25	260	3 starch, 2 fat
❦ Cool Twist Sundae Caramel	1 (6 oz.)	330	59	6	8	4	20	280	4 starch, 2 fat
❦ Cool Twist Sundae Strawberry	1 (6 oz.)	260	48	6	6	3	14	100	3 starch, 1 fat

JACK IN THE BOX

Sandwiches

Products	SERVING SIZE	CALORIES	CARBO-HYDRATE (gm)	PROTEIN (gm)	FAT (gm)	SAT. FAT (gm)	CHOLES-TEROL (mg)	SODIUM (mg)	Exchanges
Hamburger	1 (3.4 oz.)	267	28	13	11	4	26	556	2 starch, 1 med. fat meat, 1 fat
Cheeseburger	1 (4 oz.)	315	33	15	14	6	41	746	2 starch, 1 med. fat meat, 2 fat
Double Cheeseburger	1 (5.25 oz.)	467	33	21	27	12	72	842	2 starch, 2 med. fat meat, 3½ fat
Jumbo Jack	1 (7.8 oz.)	584	42	26	34	11	73	733	3 starch, 2½ med. fat meat, 4 fat

Products	SERVING SIZE	CALORIES	CARBO-HYDRATE (gm)	PROTEIN (gm)	FAT (gm)	SAT. FAT (gm)	CHOLES-TEROL (mg)	SODIUM (mg)	Exchanges
Jumbo Jack w/Cheese	1 (8.5 oz.)	667	46	32	40	14	102	1090	3 starch, 3½ med. fat meat, 4 fat
Old Fashioned Patty Melt	1 (7.5 oz.)	713	42	33	46	15	92	1360	3 starch, 3½ med. fat meat, 5 fat
Bacon Cheeseburger	1 (8.5 oz.)	705	41	35	45	15	113	1240	3 starch, 3½ med. fat meat, 5 fat
Grilled Sourdough Burger	1 (8 oz.)	712	34	32	50	16	109	1140	2 starch, 4 med. fat meat, 6 fat
Ultimate Cheeseburger	1 (10 oz.)	942	33	47	69	26	127	1176	2 starch, 6 med. fat meat, 8 fat
Chicken Fajita Pita	1 (6.6 oz.)	292	29	24	8	3	34	703	2 starch, 2½ lean meat
Chicken & Mushroom Sandwich	1 (7.8 oz.)	438	40	28	18	5	61	1340	2½ starch, 3 med. fat meat
Chicken Supreme	1 (8.6 oz.)	641	47	27	39	10	85	1470	3 starch, 2½ med. fat meat, 5 fat
Country Fried Steak Sandwich	1 (5.4 oz.)	450	42	14	25	7	36	891	3 starch, 1 med. 3 fat
Fish Supreme	1 (7.7 oz.)	510	44	24	27	6	55	1040	3 starch, 2 med. fat meat, 3 fat
Grilled Chicken Fillet	1 (7.5 oz.)	431	36	29	19	5	65	1070	2½ starch, 3 med. fat meat
Sirloin Steak Sandwich	1 (8.4 oz.)	517	49	29	23	5	66	1050	3 starch, 3 med. fat meat, 1 fat
Side Orders									
Seasoned Curly Fries	1 (3.8 oz.)	358	39	5	20	5	0	1030	2½ starch, 4 fat
French Fries	Small (2.4 oz.)	219	28	3	11	3	0	121	2 starch, 2 fat
French Fries	Regular (3.8 oz.)	351	45	4	17	4	0	194	3 starch, 3 fat
French Fries	Jumbo (4.8 oz.)	396	51	5	19	5	0	219	3½ starch, 3 fat
Onion Rings	1 (3.6 oz.)	380	38	5	23	6	0	451	2½ starch, 4 fat
Sesame Breadsticks	1 (.5 oz.)	70	12	2	2	tr	tr	110	1 starch

冐 = More than 2 fat exchanges per serving   ⵍ = More than 800 milligrams sodium   ♥ = High amounts of sugar

Products	SERVING SIZE	CALORIES	CARBO-HYDRATE (gm)	PROTEIN (gm)	FAT (gm)	SAT. FAT (gm)	CHOLES-TEROL (mg)	SODIUM (mg)	Exchanges
Tortilla Chips	1 (1 oz.)	139	18	2	6	tr	tr	134	1 starch, 1 fat
Salads/Salad Dressings									
Chef Salad	1 (11.7 oz.)	325	10	30	18	8	142	900	2 vegetable, 4 med. fat meat
Taco Salad	1 (14 oz.)	503	28	34	31	13	92	1600	2 starch, 4 med. fat meat, 1 fat
Side Salad	1 (4 oz.)	51	tr	7	3	2	tr	84	1 lean meat
Buttermilk House	2.5 oz.	362	8	tr	36	6	21	694	½ starch, 7 fat
Bleu Cheese	2.5 oz.	262	14	tr	22	4	18	918	1 starch, 4 fat
Thousand Island	2.5 oz.	312	12	tr	30	5	23	700	1 starch, 5 fat
Low Calorie Italian	2.5 oz.	25	2	tr	2	tr	0	810	Free
Mexican Food									
Taco	1 (2.75 oz.)	187	15	7	11	4	18	414	1 starch, 1 med. fat meat, 1 fat
Super Taco	1 (4.5 oz.)	281	22	12	17	6	29	718	1½ starch, 1 med. fat meat, 2 fat
Guacamole	1 pkg. (1 oz.)	30	2	1	3	tr	0	128	½ fat
Salsa	1 pkg. (1 oz.)	8	2	tr	tr	0	0	27	Free
Finger Foods									
Egg Rolls	3 piece (5.8 oz.)	437	54	3	24	7	29	957	3½ starch, 4 fat
Egg Rolls	5 piece (10 oz.)	753	92	5	41	12	49	1640	6 starch, 6 fat
Chicken Strips	4 piece (4 oz.)	285	18	25	13	3	52	695	1 starch, 3 med. fat meat
Chicken Strips	6 piece (6.25 oz.)	451	28	39	20	5	82	1100	2 starch, 4 med. fat meat
Chicken Wings	6 piece (7.25 oz.)	846	78	34	44	11	181	1710	5 starch, 3 med. fat meat, 5 fat
Chicken Wings	9 piece (11 oz.)	1270	117	51	66	16	272	2560	7 starch, 4 med. fat meat, 9 fat

Products	SERVING SIZE	CALORIES	CARBO-HYDRATE (gm)	PROTEIN (gm)	FAT (gm)	SAT. FAT (gm)	CHOLES-TEROL (mg)	SODIUM (mg)	Exchanges
▤ Mini Chimichangas	4 piece (7.3 oz.)	571	57	22	28	9	64	633	3½ starch, 2 med. fat meat, 3 fat
▤ ☀ Mini Chimichangas	6 piece (11 oz.)	856	85	34	42	13	95	949	5 starch, 3 med. fat meat, 5 fat
▤ Toasted Raviolis	7 piece (5.75 oz.)	537	57	15	28	8	36	639	4 starch, 5 fat
▤ ☀ Toasted Raviolis	10 piece	768	81	22	40	11	52	913	5 starch, 8 fat
Sweet & Sour Sauce	1 oz.	40	11	tr	tr	0	tr	160	1 fruit
BBQ Sauce	1 oz.	44	11	1	tr	tr	0	300	½ starch
Hot Sauce	.5 oz.	4	1	tr	0	0	0	112	Free
Italian Sauce	1.5 oz.	40	11	tr	tr	tr	tr	176	½ starch

Breakfast Items

Products	SERVING SIZE	CALORIES	CARBO-HYDRATE (gm)	PROTEIN (gm)	FAT (gm)	SAT. FAT (gm)	CHOLES-TEROL (mg)	SODIUM (mg)	Exchanges
Orange Juice	6.5 oz.	80	20	1	0	0	0	0	1 fruit
▤ ☀ Supreme Crescent	1 (5 oz.)	547	27	20	40	13	178	1053	2 starch, 2 med. fat meat, 6 fat
▤ ☀ Sausage Crescent	1 (5.5 oz.)	584	28	22	43	16	187	1012	2 starch, 2 med. fat meat, 6 fat
☀ Breakfast Jack	1 (4.5 oz.)	307	30	18	13	5	203	871	2 starch, 2 med. fat meat
▤ ☀ Pancake Platter	1 (8 oz.)	612	87	15	22	9	99	888	5½ starch, 4 fat
▤ ☀ Scrambled Egg Platter	1 (7.5 oz.)	559	50	18	32	9	378	1060	3 starch, 2 med. fat meat, 4 fat
☀ Scrambled Egg Pocket	1 (6.5 oz.)	431	31	29	21	8	354	1060	2 starch, 3 med. fat meat, 1 fat
☀ Sourdough Breakfast Sandwich	1 (5 oz.)	381	31	21	20	7	236	1120	2 starch, 2 med. fat meat, 2 fat
Hash Browns	1 (2 oz.)	156	14	1	11	3	0	312	1 starch, 2 fat

OCCASIONAL USE

Products	SERVING SIZE	CALORIES	CARBO-HYDRATE (gm)	PROTEIN (gm)	FAT (gm)	SAT. FAT (gm)	CHOLES-TEROL (mg)	SODIUM (mg)	Exchanges
♠ Pancake Syrup	(1.5 oz.)	121	30	0	0	0	0	6	2 fruit
♠ ▤ Hot Apple Turnover	1 (4 oz.)	354	48	3	19	5	0	479	2 starch, 1 fruit 3 fat

▤ = More than 2 fat exchanges per serving   ☀ = More than 800 milligrams sodium   ♠ = High amounts of sugar

Products	SERVING SIZE	CALORIES	CARBO-HYDRATE (gm)	PROTEIN (gm)	FAT (gm)	SAT. FAT (gm)	CHOLES-TEROL (mg)	SODIUM (mg)	Exchanges
♥ 𝖡 Cheesecake	1 (3.5 oz.)	309	29	8	18	9	63	208	2 starch, 3 fat
♥ Double Fudge Cake	1 (3 oz.)	288	49	4	9	2	20	259	3 starch, 1 fat
♥ Vanilla Milk Shake	1 (11 oz.)	320	57	10	6	4	25	230	4 starch
♥ Chocolate Milk Shake	1 (11.4 oz.)	330	55	11	7	4	25	270	4 starch
♥ Strawberry Milk Shake	1 (11.6 oz.)	320	55	10	7	4	25	240	4 starch

KFC

Original Recipe Chicken

Products	SERVING SIZE	CALORIES	CARBO-HYDRATE (gm)	PROTEIN (gm)	FAT (gm)	SAT. FAT (gm)	CHOLES-TEROL (mg)	SODIUM (mg)	Exchanges
Wing	1 (1.9 oz.)	172	5	12	11	3	59	383	½ starch, 1½ med. fat meat, ½ fat
Side Breast	1 (2.9 oz.)	245	9	18	15	4	78	604	½ starch, 2½ med. fat meat, ½ fat
Center Breast	1 (3.6 oz.)	260	8	25	14	4	92	609	½ starch, 3 med. fat meat
Drumstick	1 (2 oz.)	162	3	14	9	2	75	269	2 med. fat meat
Thigh	1 (3.4 oz.)	287	8	18	21	5	112	591	½ starch, 2 med. fat meat, 2 fat
Extra Crispy Chicken Wing	1 (2 oz.)	231	8	11	17	4	63	319	½ starch, 1½ med. fat meat, 2 fat
𝖡 Side Breast	1 (3.7 oz.)	379	16	19	27	7	77	646	1 starch, 2 med. fat meat, 3½ fat
Center Breast	1 (3.9 oz.)	344	15	23	21	5	80	636	1 starch, 3 med. fat meat, 1 fat
Drumstick	1 (2.4 oz.)	205	7	14	14	3	72	292	½ starch, 2 med. fat meat, ½ fat
𝖡 Thigh	1 (4.2 oz.)	414	14	20	31	8	112	580	1 starch, 2 med. fat meat, 4 fat

Hot & Spicy Chicken

Products	SERVING SIZE	CALORIES	CARBO-HYDRATE (gm)	PROTEIN (gm)	FAT (gm)	SAT. FAT (gm)	CHOLES-TEROL (mg)	SODIUM (mg)	Exchanges
Wing	1 (2.2 oz.)	244	9	12	18	4	65	459	½ starch, 1½ med. fat meat, 2 fat

Products	SERVING SIZE	CALORIES	CARBO-HYDRATE (gm)	PROTEIN (gm)	FAT (gm)	SAT. FAT (gm)	CHOLES-TEROL (mg)	SODIUM (mg)	Exchanges
Side Breast	1 (4.1 oz.)	398	18	21	27	7	83	922	1 starch, 2½ med. fat meat, 3 fat
Center Breast	1 (4.3 oz.)	382	16	24	25	6	84	905	1 starch, 3 med. fat meat, 2 fat
Drumstick	1 (2.5 oz.)	207	10	11	14	3	75	406	1 starch, 1 med. fat meat, 1 fat
Thigh	1 (4.2 oz.)	412	16	19	30	8	105	750	1 starch, 2 med. fat meat. 4 fat

KFC Skinfree Crispy Chicken

Products	SERVING SIZE	CALORIES	CARBO-HYDRATE (gm)	PROTEIN (gm)	FAT (gm)	SAT. FAT (gm)	CHOLES-TEROL (mg)	SODIUM (mg)	Exchanges
Center Breast	1 (4 oz.)	296	11	24	16	3	59	435	1 starch, 3 med. fat meat
Drumstick	1 (2 oz.)	166	8	13	9	2	42	256	½ starch, 2 med. fat meat
Side Breast	1 (3.6 oz.)	293	11	22	17	4	83	410	1 starch, 3 med. fat meat
Thigh	1 (3 oz.)	256	9	17	17	4	68	394	½ starch, 2 med. fat meat, 1 fat

Kentucky Nuggets and Sauces

Products	SERVING SIZE	CALORIES	CARBO-HYDRATE (gm)	PROTEIN (gm)	FAT (gm)	SAT. FAT (gm)	CHOLES-TEROL (mg)	SODIUM (mg)	Exchanges
Kentucky Nuggets	6 (3.4 oz.)	284	15	16	18	4	66	865	1 starch, 2 med. fat meat, 1 fat
Barbeque Sauce	1 oz.	35	7	tr	1	0	tr	450	½ starch or fruit
Sweet & Sour Sauce	1 oz.	58	13	tr	1	0	tr	148	1 starch or fruit
Mustard Sauce	1 oz.	36	6	1	1	0	tr	346	½ starch or fruit

Side Orders

Products	SERVING SIZE	CALORIES	CARBO-HYDRATE (gm)	PROTEIN (gm)	FAT (gm)	SAT. FAT (gm)	CHOLES-TEROL (mg)	SODIUM (mg)	Exchanges
Chicken Littles Sandwich	1 (1.7 oz.)	169	14	6	10	2	18	331	1 starch, ½ med. fat meat, 1 fat
Colonel's Chicken Sandwich	1 (5.9 oz.)	482	39	21	27	6	47	1060	2½ starch, 2 med. fat meat, 3 fat
Hot Wings	6 (4.8 oz.)	471	18	27	33	8	150	1230	1 starch, 3 med. fat meat, 4 fat
Buttermilk Biscuits	1 (2.3 oz.)	235	28	5	12	3	1	655	2 starch, 2 fat

B = More than 2 fat exchanges per serving   ☀ = More than 800 milligrams sodium   ♣ = High amounts of sugar

Products	SERVING SIZE	CALORIES	CARBO-HYDRATE (gm)	PROTEIN (gm)	FAT (gm)	SAT. FAT (gm)	CHOLES-TEROL (mg)	SODIUM (mg)	Exchanges
Mashed Potatoes w/Gravy	1 (3.5 oz.)	71	12	3	2	0	tr	339	1 starch
French Fries	1 (2.7 oz.)	244	31	3	12	3	2	139	2 starch, 2 fat
Crispy Fries	1 (3.1 oz.)	294	33	4	17	4	3	761	2 starch, 3 fat
Potato Salad	1 (3 oz.)	141	13	2	9	NA	NA	396	1 starch, 2 fat
Baked Beans	1 (3 oz.)	105	18	5	1	NA	NA	387	1 starch
Corn-on-the-Cob	1 (2.6 oz.)	90	16	3	2	1	tr	11	1 starch
Cole Slaw	1 (3.2 oz.)	114	13	1	6	1	4	177	2 vegetable or 1 starch, 1 fat

LONG JOHN SILVER'S

Meals

Products	SERVING SIZE	CALORIES	CARBO-HYDRATE (gm)	PROTEIN (gm)	FAT (gm)	SAT. FAT (gm)	CHOLES-TEROL (mg)	SODIUM (mg)	Exchanges
Fish & Fries, 2 hushpuppies, & slaw	2 pc. Fish (14.4 oz.)	890	92	31	48	10	75	1790	5 starch, 1 vegetable, 3 med. fat meat, 6 fat
Fish & Fries 2 hushpuppies	2 pc. Fish (9.2 oz.)	610	52	27	37	8	60	1480	3½ starch, 3 med. fat meat, 3 fat
Chicken Planks w/fries & slaw 2 hushpuppies	3 pc. (14.1 oz.)	890	101	32	44	10	55	2000	6 starch, 2 vegetable, 3 med. fat meat, 4 fat
Chicken Planks & Fries	2 pc. (6.9 oz.)	490	50	19	26	6	30	1290	3 starch, 2 med. fat meat, 3 fat
Clam 6 oz. w/ fries & slaw, 2 hushpuppies	1 (12.7 oz.)	990	114	24	52	11	75	1830	7 starch, 1 vegetable, 2 med. fat meat, 6 fat
Battered Shrimp w/ fries & slaw 2 hushpuppies	10 pc (11.7 oz.)	840	88	18	47	10	100	1630	5 starch, 1 vegetable 2 med. fat meat, 7 fat
Fish, Chicken & Fries	1 pc. Fish 1 pc. Chicken (8.1 oz.)	550	51	23	32	7	45	1380	3 starch, 2 med. fat meat, 4 fat
Fish & Chicken w/ fries & slaw	1 pc. Fish 2 pc. Chicken (15.2 oz.)	950	102	36	49	11	75	2090	6 starch, 1 vegetable, 4 med. fat meat, 4 fat
Fish & Shrimp w/ fries & slaw,	2 pc. Fish 8 Shrimp (17.2 oz.)	1140	108	40	65	14	145	2440	6 starch, 1 vegetable, 4 med. fat meat, 8 fat

Products	SERVING SIZE	CALORIES	CARBO-HYDRATE (gm)	PROTEIN (gm)	FAT (gm)	SAT. FAT (gm)	CHOLES-TEROL (mg)	SODIUM (mg)	Exchanges
ⓑ ⓨ Shrimp, Fish, Chicken w/ fries & slaw,	2 pc. Fish 5 Shrimp 1 pc. Chicken (18.1 oz.)	1160	113	45	65	14	135	2590	7 starch, 1 vegetable, 4½ med. fat meat, 6 fat
ⓑ ⓨ Fish, Shrimp, & Clams w/fries & slaw	2 pc. Fish 4 Shrimp 3 oz. Clams (18.1 oz.)	1240	123	44	70	15	140	2630	7 starch, 2 vegetable, 4 med. fat meat, 8 fat
ⓨ Baked Fish w/Lemon Crumb, Rice, Green Beans, Slaw, Roll	3 pc. Fish (17.4 oz.)	570	80	39	12	2	124	1470	4 starch, 2 vegetable, 4 lean meat,
Light Portion Fish w/Lemon Crumb, Rice, Salad	2 pc. Fish (9.8 oz.)	270	37	23	5	1	75	680	2 starch, 1 vegetable, 2 lean meat
ⓨ Baked Chicken Rice, Green Beans, Slaw, Roll	1 meal (16 oz.)	550	76	32	15	3	75	1670	4 starch, 2 vegetable 3 med. fat meat

Sandwiches

Products	SERVING SIZE	CALORIES	CARBO-HYDRATE (gm)	PROTEIN (gm)	FAT (gm)	SAT. FAT (gm)	CHOLES-TEROL (mg)	SODIUM (mg)	Exchanges
ⓨ Batter-dipped Fish	1 pc. Fish (5.6 oz.)	340	40	18	13	3	30	890	2½ starch, 2 med. fat meat
Batter-dipped Chicken	1 pc. Chicken (4.5 oz.)	280	39	14	8	2	15	790	2½ starch, 1 med. fat meat

Kid's Meals

Products	SERVING SIZE	CALORIES	CARBO-HYDRATE (gm)	PROTEIN (gm)	FAT (gm)	SAT. FAT (gm)	CHOLES-TEROL (mg)	SODIUM (mg)	Exchanges
ⓑ ⓨ Fish & Fries 1 hushpuppy	1 pc. Fish (7 oz.)	500	50	16	28	6	30	1010	3 starch, 1 med. fat meat, 4 fat
ⓨ Chicken Planks & Fries	2 pc. (7.8 oz.)	560	60	21	29	6	30	1310	4 starch, 2 med. fat meat, 2 fat
ⓑ ⓨ Fish, Chicken & Fries	1 pc. Fish 1 Chicken (8.9 oz.)	620	61	24	34	7	45	1400	4 starch, 2 med. fat meat, 4 fat

Salads

Products	SERVING SIZE	CALORIES	CARBO-HYDRATE (gm)	PROTEIN (gm)	FAT (gm)	SAT. FAT (gm)	CHOLES-TEROL (mg)	SODIUM (mg)	Exchanges
ⓑ ⓨ Seafood Salad without crackers	1 (9.8 oz.)	380	12	15	31	5	55	980	2 vegetable, 2 med. fat meat, 4 fat

ⓑ = More than 2 fat exchanges per serving   ⓨ = More than 800 milligrams sodium   ✿ = High amounts of sugar

Products	SERVING SIZE	CALORIES	CARBO-HYDRATE (gm)	PROTEIN (gm)	FAT (gm)	SAT. FAT (gm)	CHOLES-TEROL (mg)	SODIUM (mg)	Exchanges
Ocean Chef Salad without crackers	1 (8.3 oz.)	110	13	12	1	tr	40	730	2 vegetable, 2 lean meat
Small Salad	1 (2.4 oz.)	14	3	tr	tr	tr	0	10	1 vegetable
Finger Foods									
Batter-Dipped Fish	1 pc. (3.1 oz.)	180	12	12	11	3	30	490	1 starch, 1 med. fat meat, 1 fat
Chicken Planks	2 pc. (4 oz.)	240	22	16	12	3	30	790	1½ starch, 2 med. fat meat
A La Carte									
Battered Fish	1 pc. (3.1 oz.)	180	12	12	11	3	30	490	1 starch, 1 med. fat meat, 1 fat
Chicken Plank	1 pc. (2 oz.)	120	11	8	6	2	15	400	1 starch, 1 med. fat meat
Breaded Shrimp	1 pc. (.4 oz.)	30	2	1	2	tr	10	80	Free
Baked Fish w/Lemon Crumb	3 pc. (5 oz.)	150	4	29	1	tr	110	370	3 lean meat
Chicken Light Herb	1 pc. (3.5 oz.)	120	tr	22	4	1	60	570	3 lean meat
Seafood Gumbo w/Cod	1 order (7 oz.)	120	4	9	8	2	25	740	1 vegetable, 1 med. fat meat
Seafood Chowder w/Cod	1 order (7 oz.)	140	10	11	6	2	20	590	1 starch, 1 med. fat meat
Fries	1 order (3 oz.)	220	28	3	15	3	0	500	2 starch, 2 fat
Hushpuppies	1 pc.	70	10	2	2	tr	5	25	½ starch, ½ fat
Cole Slaw	1 order	140	20	1	6	1	15	260	1 starch, 1 fat
Corn Cobbette	1 pc. (3.3 oz.)	140	18	3	8	1	0	0	1 starch, 1½ fat
Green Beans	1 order (3.5 oz.)	20	3	1	tr	tr	0	320	1 vegetable
Rice	1 order (4 oz.)	160	30	3	3	tr	0	340	2 starch
Roll	1 (1.5 oz.)	110	23	4	tr	tr	0	170	1½ starch

Products	SERVING SIZE	CALORIES	CARBO-HYDRATE (gm)	PROTEIN (gm)	FAT (gm)	SAT. FAT (gm)	CHOLES-TEROL (mg)	SODIUM (mg)	Exchanges
Condiments/Salad Dressings									
Seafood Sauce	½ oz.	14	3	tr	tr	0	0	180	Free
Tartar Sauce	½ oz.	50	2	tr	5	1	0	35	1 fat
🗎 Ranch Dressing	1 oz.	180	tr	tr	19	4	5	230	4 fat
Creamy Italian Dressing	1 oz.	30	tr	tr	3	tr	tr	280	1 fat
🗎 Sea Salad Dressing	1 oz.	140	2	tr	15	6	5	160	3 fat
OCCASIONAL USE									
🍬 Apple Pie	4.5 oz.	320	43	3	13	5	5	420	3 starch, 2 fat
🍬 Cherry Pie	4.5 oz.	360	55	4	13	4	5	200	3½ starch, 2 fat
🍬 Lemon Pie	4 oz.	340	60	7	9	3	45	130	4 starch, 1 fat
🗎🍬 Walnut Brownie	3.4 oz.	440	54	5	22	5	20	150	3½ starch, 4 fat
🍬 Oatmeal Raisin Cookie	1.8 oz.	160	15	3	10	2	15	150	1 starch, 2 fat
🍬 Chocolate Chip Cookie	1.8 oz.	230	35	3	9	6	10	170	2 starch, 2 fat

MCDONALD'S

Products	SERVING SIZE	CALORIES	CARBO-HYDRATE (gm)	PROTEIN (gm)	FAT (gm)	SAT. FAT (gm)	CHOLES-TEROL (mg)	SODIUM (mg)	Exchanges
Sandwiches									
Hamburger	1 (3.6 oz.)	255	30	12	9	3	37	490	2 starch, 1 med. fat meat, 1 fat
Cheeseburger	1 (4 oz.)	305	30	15	13	5	50	725	2 starch, 1½ med. fat meat, 1 fat
Quarter Pounder	1 (5.9 oz.)	410	34	23	20	8	85	645	2 starch, 3 med. fat meat, 1 fat
🍴 Quarter Pounder w/Cheese	1 (6.8 oz.)	510	34	28	28	11	115	1110	2 starch, 3½ med. fat meat, 2 fat
🍴 Big Mac	1 (7.6 oz.)	500	42	25	26	9	100	890	3 starch, 2½ med. fat meat, 2 fat
Filet-O-Fish	1 (5 oz.)	370	38	14	18	4	50	730	2½ starch, 1 med. fat meat, 2 fat

🗎 = More than 2 fat exchanges per serving   🍴 = More than 800 milligrams sodium   🍬 = High amounts of sugar

Products	SERVING SIZE	CALORIES	CARBO-HYDRATE (gm)	PROTEIN (gm)	FAT (gm)	SAT. FAT (gm)	CHOLES-TEROL (mg)	SODIUM (mg)	Exchanges
McLean Deluxe	1 (7.3 oz.)	320	35	22	10	4	60	670	2 starch, 3 lean meat
McLean Deluxe with Cheese	1 (7.7 oz.)	370	35	24	14	5	75	890	2 starch, 3 lean meat, 1 fat
McChicken	1 (6.5 oz.)	415	39	19	20	4	50	830	2½ starch, 2 med. fat meat, 2 fat
Chicken Fajitas	1 (2.9 oz.)	190	20	11	8	2	35	310	1 starch, 1 lean meat, 1 fat

Chicken McNuggets/Sauces

Products	SERVING SIZE	CALORIES	CARBO-HYDRATE (gm)	PROTEIN (gm)	FAT (gm)	SAT. FAT (gm)	CHOLES-TEROL (mg)	SODIUM (mg)	Exchanges
Chicken McNuggets	4 piece (2.6 oz.)	180	11	13	10	2	35	390	1 starch, 1½ med. fat meat
Chicken McNuggets	6 piece (3.9 oz.)	270	17	20	15	4	55	580	1 starch, 2 med. fat meat, 1 fat
Chicken McNuggets	9 piece (5.9 oz.)	405	25	30	22	5	85	870	1½ starch, 3 med. fat meat, 1½ fat
Hot Mustard Sauce	1 (1 oz.)	70	8	0	4	tr	5	250	½ fruit, ½ fat
Barbeque Sauce	1 (1.1 oz.)	50	12	0	tr	0	0	340	1 fruit
Sweet and Sour Sauce	1 (1.1 oz.)	60	14	0	tr	0	0	190	1 fruit

Pizza, 12" Family Size

Products	SERVING SIZE	CALORIES	CARBO-HYDRATE (gm)	PROTEIN (gm)	FAT (gm)	SAT. FAT (gm)	CHOLES-TEROL (mg)	SODIUM (mg)	Exchanges
Cheese	1 slice (2.6 oz.)	178	24	10	7	3	14	399	1½ starch, 1 med. fat meat
Deluxe	1 slice (3.4 oz.)	216	24	10	8	4	20	549	1½ starch, 1 med. fat meat
Pepperoni	1 slice (2.8 oz.)	208	23	10	7	3	18	523	1½ starch, 1 med. fat meat
Sausage	1 slice (3 oz.)	216	23	10	8	4	22	530	1½ starch, 1 med. fat meat

French Fries

Products	SERVING SIZE	CALORIES	CARBO-HYDRATE (gm)	PROTEIN (gm)	FAT (gm)	SAT. FAT (gm)	CHOLES-TEROL (mg)	SODIUM (mg)	Exchanges
French Fries	Small (2.4 oz.)	220	26	3	12	3	0	110	2 starch, 2 fat
French Fries	Medium (3.4 oz.)	320	36	4	17	4	0	150	2½ starch, 3 fat
French Fries	Large (4.3 oz.)	400	46	6	22	5	0	200	3 starch, 4 fat

Products	SERVING SIZE	CALORIES	CARBO-HYDRATE (gm)	PROTEIN (gm)	FAT (gm)	SAT. FAT (gm)	CHOLES-TEROL (mg)	SODIUM (mg)	Exchanges
Salads									
Chef Salad	1 (9.3 oz.)	170	8	17	9	4	111	400	1 vegetable, 2 med. fat meat
Garden Salad	1 (6.6 oz.)	50	6	4	2	tr	65	70	1 vegetable
Chunky Chicken Salad	1 (9 oz.)	150	7	25	4	1	78	230	1 vegetable, 3 lean meat
Side Salad	1 (3.7 oz.)	30	4	2	1	tr	33	85	1 vegetable
Croutons	.4 oz.	50	7	1	2	1	0	140	½ starch
Bacon Bits	.1 oz.	15	0	1	1	tr	1	95	Free
Salad Dressings									
Blue Cheese	.5 oz.	50	1	0	4	1	7	150	1 fat
	2.5 oz. packet	225	5	0	20	5	35	750	5 fat
Ranch	.5 oz.	55	1	0	5	1	5	130	1 fat
	2 oz. packet	220	4	0	25	5	25	650	5 fat
1000 Island	.5 oz.	45	4	0	3	1	8	100	1 fat
	2.5 oz.	225	20	0	15	5	40	500	5 fat
Lite Vinaigrette	.5 oz.	12	2	0	1	tr	0	60	Free
	2 oz. packet	48	8	0	4	1	0	240	1 fat
Red French Reduced Calorie	.5 oz.	40	5	0	2	tr	0	115	1 fat
	2 oz. packet	160	20	0	9	1	0	460	1 starch, 2 fat
Breakfast									
Egg McMuffin	1 (4.8 oz.)	280	28	18	11	4	235	710	2 starch, 2 med. fat meat
Sausage McMuffin	1 (4.8 oz.)	345	27	15	20	7	57	770	2 starch, 1½ med. fat meat, 2 fat
Sausage McMuffin w/Egg	1 (5.6 oz.)	430	27	21	25	3	270	920	2 starch, 2½ med. fat meat, 2 fat
Scrambled Eggs	2 (3.5 oz.)	140	1	12	10	3	425	290	2 med. fat meat
Sausage	1 (1.5 oz.)	160	0	7	15	5	43	310	1 med. fat meat, 2 fat
English Muffin with Spread	1 (2 oz.)	170	26	5	4	1	0	285	2 starch, 1 fat
Hash Brown Potatoes	1 (1.9 oz.)	130	15	1	7	2	1	330	1 starch, 1 fat

8 = More than 2 fat exchanges per serving   ☀ = More than 800 milligrams sodium   ♥ = High amounts of sugar

Products	SERVING SIZE	CALORIES	CARBO-HYDRATE (gm)	PROTEIN (gm)	FAT (gm)	SAT. FAT (gm)	CHOLES-TEROL (mg)	SODIUM (mg)	Exchanges
Biscuit with Biscuit Spread	1 (2.6 oz.)	260	32	5	13	3	1	730	2 starch, 2 fat
Sausage Biscuit	1 (4.2 oz.)	420	32	12	28	8	44	1040	2 starch, 1 med. fat meat, 4 fat
Sausage Biscuit with Egg	1 (6.2 oz.)	505	33	19	33	10	260	1210	2 starch, 2 med. meat, 4 fat
Bacon, Egg and Cheese Biscuit	1 (5.4 oz.)	440	33	15	26	8	240	1215	2 starch, 2 med. fat meat, 3 fat
Breakfast Burrito	1 (3.7 oz.)	280	21	12	17	4	135	580	1½ starch, 1 med. fat meat, 2 fat
Cheerios	¾ cup	80	14	3	1	tr	0	210	1 starch
Wheaties	¾ cup	90	19	2	1	tr	0	220	1 starch
Fat-Free Apple Bran	1 (2.6 oz.)	180	40	5	0	0	0	200	2½ starch
Hot Cakes (plain)	1 order	250	44	8	3	2	8	570	3 starch, ½ fat
Margarine	2 pats	70	0	0	8	2	0	110	1½ fat
Syrup	1½ fl. oz.	120	30	0	0	0	0	5	2 fruit
Orange, Grapefruit or Apple Juice	6 oz.	80	19	1	0	0	0	0	1 fruit

OCCASIONAL USE

Products	SERVING SIZE	CALORIES	CARBO-HYDRATE (gm)	PROTEIN (gm)	FAT (gm)	SAT. FAT (gm)	CHOLES-TEROL (mg)	SODIUM (mg)	Exchanges
Baked Apple Pie	1 (3 oz.)	280	35	3	15	2	0	90	1 starch, 1 fruit, 3 fat
McDonaldland Cookies	1 box (2 oz.)	290	47	4	7	1	0	300	3 starch, 1 fat
Chocolate Chip Cookies	1 box (2 oz.)	330	42	4	15	4	4	280	2½ starch, 3 fat
Vanilla Lowfat Frozen Yogurt Cone	1 (3 oz.)	105	22	4	1	tr	3	80	1½ starch
Strawberry Lowfat Frozen Yogurt Sundae	1 (6 oz.)	210	49	6	1	tr	5	95	2 starch, 1 fruit
Hot Fudge Frozen Yogurt Sundae	1 (6 oz.)	240	50	7	3	2	6	170	2 starch, 1½ fruit
Hot Caramel Frozen Yogurt Sundae	1 (6 oz.)	270	59	7	3	2	13	180	2 starch, 2 fruit
Vanilla Lowfat Milk Shake	1 (10.4 oz.)	290	60	11	1	tr	10	170	4 starch

Products	SERVING SIZE	CALORIES	CARBO-HYDRATE (gm)	PROTEIN (gm)	FAT (gm)	SAT. FAT (gm)	CHOLES-TEROL (mg)	SODIUM (mg)	Exchanges
♥ Chocolate Lowfat Milk Shake	1 (10.4 oz.)	320	66	11	2	1	10	240	4 starch
♥ Strawberry Lowfat Milk Shake	1 (10.4 oz.)	320	67	11	1	tr	10	170	4 starch
🍴 ♥ Apple Danish	1 (4 oz.)	390	51	6	17	4	25	370	3 starch, 3 fat
🍴 ♥ Iced Cheese Danish	1 (3.9 oz.)	390	42	7	21	6	47	420	3 starch, 4 fat
🍴 ♥ Cinnamon Raisin Danish	1 (3.9 oz.)	440	58	6	21	5	34	430	4 starch, 3 fat
🍴 ♥ Raspberry Danish	1 (4.1 oz.)	410	62	6	16	3	26	310	4 starch, 2 fat

MRS. WINNER'S CHICKEN & BISCUITS

Specialties

Biscuit	1 (2.3 oz.)	245	45	4	5	NA	tr	503	3 starch, 1 fat
Sausage Patties	1 (1.3 oz.)	200	tr	6	10	NA	8	400	1 high fat meat, 1 fat
Country Ham	1 (1 oz.)	60	tr	4	1	NA	14	565	1 lean meat
Baked Chicken Fillet	1 (3 oz.)	120	tr	10	2	NA	33	360	2 lean meat
Country Fried Steak	1 (2.2 oz.)	220	tr	12	14	NA	7	205	2 med. fat meat 1 fat
Seafood Salad	1 (13 oz.)	553	41	5	9	NA	4	756	3 starch, 2 fat
☂ Chicken Salad	1 (13.7 oz.)	583	39	9	8	NA	3	875	3 starch, 2 fat

Sandwiches

☂ Breaded Chicken Sandwich	1 (3.2 oz.)	203	12	19	10	NA	37	1000	1 starch, 2 med. fat meat
Chicken Salad Sandwich	1 (6.5 oz.)	313	33	10	6	NA	1	599	2 starch, 2 lean meat
Chicken Fillet Sandwich	1 (6.4 oz.)	379	45	12	7	NA	28	541	3 starch, 2 lean meat
Steak Sandwich	1 (6.3 oz.)	429	43	11	11	NA	21	644	3 starch, 2 med. fat meat

🍴 = More than 2 fat exchanges per serving   ☂ = More than 800 milligrams sodium   ♥ = High amounts of sugar

Products	SERVING SIZE	CALORIES	CARBO-HYDRATE (gm)	PROTEIN (gm)	FAT (gm)	SAT. FAT (gm)	CHOLES-TEROL (mg)	SODIUM (mg)	Exchanges
Side Orders									
Baked Beans	1 order (4.4 oz.)	149	31	5	tr	NA	1	436	2 starch
Cole Slaw	1 order (3.7 oz.)	188	9	1	16	NA	1	549	2 vegetable, 3 fat
Potato Fries	1 order (3.8 oz.)	225	27	6	9	NA	1	214	2 starch, 2 fat
Mashed Potatoes w/Gravy	1 order (6.1 oz.)	148	22	3	3	NA	2	823	1½ starch, 1 fat
Tossed Salad	1 (4 oz.)	6	1	1	tr	NA	1	439	1 vegetable

PIZZA HUT

Thin 'N Crispy

Products	SERVING SIZE	CALORIES	CARBO-HYDRATE (gm)	PROTEIN (gm)	FAT (gm)	SAT. FAT (gm)	CHOLES-TEROL (mg)	SODIUM (mg)	Exchanges
Cheese	1 slice of medium pizza	223	19	13	10	5	25	503	1 starch, 1½ med fat meat, 1 fat
Beef	1 slice of medium pizza	231	20	13	11	3	25	705	1 starch, 1½ med fat meat, 1 fat
Pepperoni	1 slice of medium pizza	230	20	12	11	3	27	678	1 starch, 1½ med fat meat, 1 fat
Italian Sausage	1 slice of medium pizza	282	20	14	17	6	38	781	1 starch, 1½ med fat meat, 2 fat
Pork	1 slice of medium pizza	240	20	13	12	3	25	713	1 starch, 1½ med fat meat, 1 fat
Meat Lovers	1 slice of medium pizza	297	20	14	16	4	44	1068	1 starch, 2 med fat meat, 2 fat
Veggie Lovers	1 slice of medium pizza	192	20	11	8	3	17	551	1 starch, 1½ med fat meat
Pepperoni Lovers	1 slice of medium pizza	320	20	18	19	4	46	949	1 starch, 2 med fat meat, 2 fat
Supreme	1 slice of medium pizza	262	20	15	14	3	31	819	1 starch, 2 med fat meat, 1 fat
Super Supreme	1 slice of medium pizza	253	20	16	12	3	35	700	1 starch, 2 med fat meat, ½ fat

Products	SERVING SIZE	CALORIES	CARBO-HYDRATE (gm)	PROTEIN (gm)	FAT (gm)	SAT. FAT (gm)	CHOLES-TEROL (mg)	SODIUM (mg)	Exchanges
Hand Tossed									
Cheese	1 slice of medium pizza	253	27	15	9	4	25	593	2 starch, 1½ med fat meat
Beef	1 slice of medium pizza	261	28	15	10	3	25	795	2 starch, 1½ med fat meat
Pepperoni	1 slice of medium pizza	283	28	20	10	3	25	738	2 starch, 2 med fat meat
ⵌ Italian Sausage	1 slice of medium pizza	313	27	16	15	6	38	871	2 starch, 1½ med fat meat, 1 fat
ⵌ Pork	1 slice of medium pizza	270	28	15	11	3	25	803	2 starch, 1½ med fat meat
ⵌ Meat Lovers	1 slice of medium pizza	321	28	16	15	4	42	1106	2 starch, 1½ med fat meat, 1 fat
Veggie Lovers	1 slice of medium pizza	222	28	13	7	3	17	641	2 starch, 1½ lean meat
ⵌ Pepperoni Lovers	1 slice of medium pizza	335	28	19	16	4	43	981	2 starch, 2 med fat meat, 1 fat
ⵌ Supreme	1 slice of medium pizza	289	28	17	12	3	29	894	2 starch, 1½ med fat meat, ½ fat
ⵌ Super Supreme	1 slice of medium pizza	276	28	17	10	3	32	980	2 starch, 1½ med fat meat
Pan									
Cheese	1 slice of medium pizza	279	26	14	13	5	35	473	2 starch, 1½ med fat meat, 1 fat
Beef	1 slice of medium pizza	288	27	10	18	3	25	675	2 starch, 1 med fat meat, 2 fat
Pepperoni	1 slice of medium pizza	280	26	8	18	3	25	618	2 starch, I med fat meat, 2 fat
▤ Italian Sausage	1 slice of medium pizza	399	26	15	24	6	38	751	2 starch, 1½ med fat meat, 3 fat
Pork	1 slice of medium pizza	296	27	10	19	3	25	683	2 starch, 1 med fat meat, 2 fat
ⵌ Meat Lovers	1 slice of medium pizza	347	27	15	23	5	42	986	2 starch, 1½ med fat meat, 2 fat
Veggie Lovers	1 slice of medium pizza	249	27	7	15	3	17	521	2 starch, 2 fat

▤ = More than 2 fat exchanges per serving   ⵌ = More than 800 milligrams sodium   ♥ = High amounts of sugar

Products	SERVING SIZE	CALORIES	CARBO-HYDRATE (gm)	PROTEIN (gm)	FAT (gm)	SAT. FAT (gm)	CHOLES-TEROL (mg)	SODIUM (mg)	Exchanges
Pepperoni Lovers	1 slice of medium pizza	362	27	14	25	5	34	861	2 starch, 1½ med fat meat, 3 fat
Supreme	1 slice of medium pizza	315	27	16	16	3	29	774	2 starch, 1½ med fat meat, 1 fat
Super Supreme	1 slice of medium pizza	302	27	12	19	4	32	860	2 starch, 1 med fat meat, 2 fat
Bigfoot									
Cheese	1 slice	179	24	9	5	3	14	959	1½ starch, 1 med fat meat
Pepperoni	1 slice	195	24	10	7	3	17	1022	1½ starch, 1 med fat meat
Pepperoni, Italian Sausage, Mushroom	1 slice	213	25	10	8	4	21	1208	1½ starch, I med fat meat, ½ fat
Personal Pan Pizza									
Pepperoni	1 whole	675	76	36	29	NA	53	1335	5 starch, 3 med fat meat, 2 fat
Supreme	1 whole	647	76	37	28	NA	53	1313	5 starch, 3 med fat meat, 1 fat

PONDEROSA

Entrees

Products	SERVING SIZE	CALORIES	CARBO-HYDRATE (gm)	PROTEIN (gm)	FAT (gm)	SAT. FAT (gm)	CHOLES-TEROL (mg)	SODIUM (mg)	Exchanges
Fish, baked									
Bake 'R Broil	5.2 oz.	230	10	19	13	NA	50	330	1 starch, 2 med. fat meat
Baked Scrod	7.0 oz.	120	0	27	1	NA	65	80	3 lean meat
Fish, broiled									
Halibut	6.0 oz.	170	0	35	3	NA	NA	68	4 lean meat
Roughy	5.0 oz.	139	0	21	5	NA	28	88	3 lean meat
Salmon	6.0 oz.	192	3	37	3	NA	60	72	4 lean meat
Swordfish	5.9 oz.	271	0	44	10	NA	84	80	5 lean meat
Trout	5.0 oz.	228	1	30	4	NA	110	51	4 lean meat
Fish, fried	3.2 oz.	190	17	9	9	NA	15	170	1 starch, 1 med. fat meat, 1 fat
Shrimp, fried	7 pieces	230	31	22	1	NA	105	612	2 starch, 2 lean meat
Chicken breast	5.5 oz.	98	1	20	2	NA	54	400	3 lean meat

Products	SERVING SIZE	CALORIES	CARBO- HYDRATE (gm)	PROTEIN (gm)	FAT (gm)	SAT. FAT (gm)	CHOLES- TEROL (mg)	SODIUM (mg)	Exchanges
Chopped steak	4.0 oz.	225	1	19	16	NA	80	150	3 med. fat meat
Chopped steak	5.3 oz.	296	1	25	22	NA	105	296	4 med. fat meat
Hot dog	1.6 oz.	144	1	5	13	NA	27	460	1 high fat meat, 1 fat
⚓ Kansas City strip	5 oz.	138	1	21	6	NA	76	850	3 lean meat
⚓ New York Strip, Choice	10 oz.	314	1	45	15	NA	50	1420	6 lean meat
New York Strip, Choice	8 oz.	304	2	34	11	NA	62	570	5 lean meat
⚓ Porterhouse, Choice	16 oz.	640	3	57	31	NA	82	1130	8 med. fat meat
⚓ Porterhouse, Non-graded	13 oz.	440	1	43	30	NA	67	1844	6 med. fat meat
Ribeye, Choice	6 oz.	282	1	29	14	NA	60	570	4 med. fat meat
⚓ Ribeye, Non-graded	5 oz.	219	1	25	13	NA	75	1130	3 med. fat meat
⚓ Sandwich Steak	4 oz.	208	2	20	11	NA	62	850	3 med. fat meat
Sirloin, Choice	7 oz.	241	1	35	11	NA	63	570	5 lean meat
Sirloin Tips, Choice	5 oz.	197	1	29	8	NA	71	280	4 lean meat
Steak Kabobs (meat only)	3 oz.	153	2	26	5	NA	67	280	3 lean meat
⚓ Teriyaki Steak	5 oz.	174	5	32	3	NA	64	1420	4 lean meat
⚓ T-Bone, Choice	10 oz.	444	2	44	18	NA	80	850	6 med. fat meat
⚓ T-Bone, Non-graded	8 oz.	277	1	35	9	NA	71	850	5 lean meat
Chicken Wings	2 pieces	213	11	11	9	NA	75	610	1 starch, 1 med. fat meat, 1 fat
Meatballs	2 pieces	115	2	5	4	NA	21	16	1 med. fat meat
Mini Shrimp	6 pieces	47	6	5	1	NA	22	125	1 lean meat

Side Orders

Products	SERVING SIZE	CALORIES	CARBO- HYDRATE (gm)	PROTEIN (gm)	FAT (gm)	SAT. FAT (gm)	CHOLES- TEROL (mg)	SODIUM (mg)	Exchanges
Sweet/Sour Sauce	1 oz.	37	8	tr	tr	NA	0	80	½ fruit
Breaded Cauliflower	4 oz.	115	23	4	1	NA	1	446	1½ starch
Breaded Okra	4 oz.	124	23	3	1	NA	1	483	1½ starch
Breaded Onion Rings	4 oz.	213	30	3	9	NA	2	620	2 starch, 2 fat
Breaded Zucchini	4 oz.	102	18	3	1	NA	1	584	1 starch

B = More than 2 fat exchanges per serving   ⚓ = More than 800 milligrams sodium   ☘ = High amounts of sugar

Products	SERVING SIZE	CALORIES	CARBO-HYDRATE (gm)	PROTEIN (gm)	FAT (gm)	SAT. FAT (gm)	CHOLES-TEROL (mg)	SODIUM (mg)	Exchanges
Cheese, Herb, Garlic	1 tbsp.	100	0	0	10	NA	0	120	2 fat
Italian Breadsticks	1 each	100	19	4	1	NA	0	200	1 starch
Potato Wedges	3.5 oz.	130	16	3	6	NA	NA	170	1 starch, 1 fat
Rice Pilaf	4 oz.	160	26	4	4	NA	22	450	1½ starch, 1 fat
Rolls, Dinner	1 each	184	33	5	3	NA	0	311	2 starch, ½ fat
Rolls, Sourdough	1 each	110	22	4	1	NA	0	230	1½ starch
Stuffing	4 oz.	230	27	6	11	NA	22	800	2 starch, 2 fat
Tortilla Chips	1 oz.	150	16	3	8	NA	0	80	1 starch, 2 fat
Spaghetti and Sauce	6 oz.	188	33	5	5	NA	0	520	2 starch, 1 med. fat meat
Beans, Baked	4 oz.	170	21	6	6	NA	0	330	1½ starch, 1 fat
Beans, Green	3.5 oz.	20	3	1	0	NA	0	391	1 vegetable
Carrots	3.5 oz.	31	7	1	0	NA	0	33	1 vegetable
Corn	3.5 oz.	90	21	3	0	NA	0	5	1½ starch
Peas	3.5 oz.	67	12	5	0	NA	0	120	1 starch
Potatoes, Baked	7.2 oz.	145	33	4	0	NA	0	6	2 starch
Potatoes, French fried	3 oz.	120	17	2	4	NA	3	39	1 starch, 1 fat
Potatoes, Mashed	4 oz.	62	13	2	0	NA	20	191	1 starch

Salad Dressings

Products	SERVING SIZE	CALORIES	CARBO-HYDRATE (gm)	PROTEIN (gm)	FAT (gm)	SAT. FAT (gm)	CHOLES-TEROL (mg)	SODIUM (mg)	Exchanges
Blue Cheese Dressing	1 oz.	130	1	1	14	NA	27	266	3 fat
Cole Slaw Dressing	1 oz.	150	6	tr	14	NA	31	284	3 fat
Creamy Italian Dressing	1 oz.	103	3	0	10	NA	0	373	2 fat
Parmesan Pepper Dressing	1 oz.	150	2	1	15	NA	9	281	3 fat
Ranch Dressing	1 oz.	147	1	tr	15	NA	3	297	3 fat
Reduced Calorie Cucumber	1 oz.	69	3	tr	6	NA	0	315	1½ fat
Reduced Calorie Italian	1 oz.	31	1	0	3	NA	0	371	1 fat
Sweet-n-Tangy Dressing	1 oz.	122	8	tr	10	NA	1	347	2 fat

Products	SERVING SIZE	CALORIES	CARBO-HYDRATE (gm)	PROTEIN (gm)	FAT (gm)	SAT. FAT (gm)	CHOLES-TEROL (mg)	SODIUM (mg)	Exchanges
Thousand Island Dressing	1 oz.	113	8	tr	10	NA	9	405	2 fat

Salad Bar

Products	SERVING SIZE	CALORIES	CARBO-HYDRATE (gm)	PROTEIN (gm)	FAT (gm)	SAT. FAT (gm)	CHOLES-TEROL (mg)	SODIUM (mg)	Exchanges
Lettuce	1 oz.	5	2	0	0	NA	0	5	Free
Raw vegetables	1 oz.	9	2	1	0	NA	0	3	Free
Cheese, Shredded Imitation	1 oz.	90	1	6	7	NA	5	420	1 high fat meat
Chicken Salad	3.5 oz.	212	8	11	15	NA	42	334	½ starch, 2 med. fat meat
Croutons	1 oz.	115	18	4	4	NA	0	351	1 starch, 1 fat
Eggs, Diced	2 oz.	93	1	7	7	NA	260	74	1 med. fat meat
Garbanzo Beans	1 oz.	102	17	6	0	NA	0	7	1 starch
Ham, Diced	2 oz.	120	1	9	10	NA	76	780	1 med. fat meat, 1 fat
Julienne Turkey	1 oz.	29	1	5	1	NA	15	192	1 lean meat
Macaroni Salad	3.5 oz.	335	49	8	12	NA	9	431	3 starch, 2 fat
Pasta Salad, pre-made	3.5 oz.	268	34	6	12	NA	0	441	2 starch, 2 fat
Potato Salad	3.5 oz.	126	16	2	6	NA	7	300	1 starch, 1 fat
Turkey Ham Salad	3.5 oz.	186	10	8	13	NA	12	654	1 starch, 1 med. fat meat, 1 fat
Cheese Spread	1 oz.	98	4	4	7	NA	26	188	1 high fat meat
Cottage Cheese	4 oz.	120	5	15	5	NA	17	330	2 lean meat
Cracker Assortment Meal Mate Sesame	2 pieces	45	6	1	2	NA	0	95	½ starch
Melba Snacks	4 pieces	36	8	2	0	NA	0	60	½ starch
Ritz	2 pieces	40	4	0	2	NA	0	50	½ starch
Sesame Breadsticks	2 pieces	35	6	1	0	NA	0	60	½ starch

OCCASIONAL USE

Products	SERVING SIZE	CALORIES	CARBO-HYDRATE (gm)	PROTEIN (gm)	FAT (gm)	SAT. FAT (gm)	CHOLES-TEROL (mg)	SODIUM (mg)	Exchanges
☗ Gelatin, Plain	4 oz.	71	17	1	0	NA	0	73	1 starch
☷ ☗ Mousse, Chocolate	4 oz.	312	28	0	18	NA	0	72	2 starch, 3 fat

☷ = More than 2 fat exchanges per serving   ☰ = More than 800 milligrams sodium   ☗ = High amounts of sugar

Products	SERVING SIZE	CALORIES	CARBO-HYDRATE (gm)	PROTEIN (gm)	FAT (gm)	SAT. FAT (gm)	CHOLES-TEROL (mg)	SODIUM (mg)	Exchanges
Mousse, Strawberry	4 oz.	297	25	0	18	NA	0	68	2 starch, 3 fat
Wafer, Vanilla	2 cookies	35	6	0	1	NA	5	25	½ starch
Yogurt, Fruit	4 oz.	115	23	5	1	NA	5	70	1½ starch
Yogurt, Vanilla	4 oz.	110	18	5	2	NA	6	75	1½ starch
Banana Pudding	4 oz.	207	27	1	10	NA	0	114	2 starch, 2 fat
Ice Milk, Chocolate	3.5 oz.	152	30	4	3	NA	22	70	2 starch
Ice Milk, Vanilla	3.5 oz.	150	30	4	3	NA	20	58	2 starch
Topping, Caramel	1 oz.	100	26	tr	1	NA	2	72	1½ fruit
Topping, Chocolate	1 oz.	90	24	tr	tr	NA	0	37	1½ fruit
Topping, Strawberry	1 oz.	71	24	tr	tr	NA	0	29	1½ fruit
Topping, Whipped	1 oz.	80	5	0	7	NA	0	16	2 fat

POPEYES

Fried Chicken

Products	SERVING SIZE	CALORIES	CARBO-HYDRATE (gm)	PROTEIN (gm)	FAT (gm)	SAT. FAT (gm)	CHOLES-TEROL (mg)	SODIUM (mg)	Exchanges
Wing, Mild or Spicy	1.6 oz.	160	7	9	11	NA	40	290	½ starch, 1 med. fat meat, 1 fat
Leg, Mild or Spicy	1.7 oz.	120	5	10	7	NA	40	240	1 med. fat meat, 1 fat
Thigh, Mild or Spicy	3.1 oz.	300	9	15	23	NA	70	620	½ starch, 2 med. fat meat, 3 fat
Breast, Mild or Spicy	3.7 oz.	270	9	23	16	NA	60	660	½ starch, 3 med. fat meat

Side Orders

Products	SERVING SIZE	CALORIES	CARBO-HYDRATE (gm)	PROTEIN (gm)	FAT (gm)	SAT. FAT (gm)	CHOLES-TEROL (mg)	SODIUM (mg)	Exchanges
Nuggets	4.2 oz.	410	18	17	32	NA	55	660	1 starch, 2 med. fat meat, 4 fat
Shrimp	2.8 oz.	250	13	16	16	NA	11	650	1 starch, 2 med. fat meat, 1 fat
Biscuits	2.3 oz.	250	26	4	15	NA	5	460	2 starch, 2 fat
Potatoes & Gravy	3.8 oz.	100	11	5	6	NA	5	460	1 starch, 1 fat
Cole Slaw	4 oz.	149	14	1	11	NA	3	271	1 starch, 2 fat
French Fries	3 oz.	240	31	4	12	NA	10	610	2 starch, 2 fat

Products	SERVING SIZE	CALORIES	CARBO-HYDRATE (gm)	PROTEIN (gm)	FAT (gm)	SAT. FAT (gm)	CHOLES-TEROL (mg)	SODIUM (mg)	Exchanges
☒ Onion Rings	3.1 oz.	310	31	5	19	NA	25	210	2 starch, 3 fat
⚕ Cajun Rice	3.9 oz.	150	17	10	5	NA	25	1260	1 starch, 1 med. fat meat
Corn on the Cob	5.2 oz.	90	21	4	3	NA	0	20	1½ starch
☒ Red Beans & Rice	5.9 oz.	270	30	8	17	NA	10	680	2 starch, 3 fat
OCCASIONAL USE									
☒☕ Apple Pie	3.1 oz.	290	37	3	16	NA	10	820	1½ starch, 1 fruit 3 fat

QUINCY'S FAMILY STEAK HOUSE

Entrees

Products	SERVING SIZE	CALORIES	CARBO-HYDRATE (gm)	PROTEIN (gm)	FAT (gm)	SAT. FAT (gm)	CHOLES-TEROL (mg)	SODIUM (mg)	Exchanges
☒ Sirloin Steak	Large (10 oz.)	852	0	50	70	NA	NA	241	7 med. fat meat, 7 fat
☒ Sirloin Steak	Regular (8 oz.)	649	0	38	54	NA	NA	206	5½ med. fat meat, 5 fat
☒ Sirloin Steak	Petite (5.5 oz.)	446	0	26	37	NA	NA	118	4 med. fat meat, 3 fat
Sirloin Club Steak	1 (6 oz.)	283	0	44	10	NA	NA	160	6 lean meat
☒ T-Bone	1 (14 oz.)	1612	0	71	159	NA	NA	389	10 med. fat meat, 22 fat
☒ Ribeye, Extra-thick	1 (13 oz.)	865	0	40	78	NA	NA	298	6 med. fat meat, 10 fat
☒ Ribeye Steak	1 (10 oz.)	665	0	31	60	NA	NA	205	4½ med. fat meat, 7½ fat
Filet	1 (7 oz.)	331	0	40	12	NA	NA	159	6 lean meat
Sirloin Tips	1 order (4 oz.)	236	0	37	9	NA	NA	113	5 lean meat
Chopped Steak	1 (5.75 oz.)	466	0	40	34	NA	NA	96	5½ med. fat meat, 1 fat
Luncheon Chopped Steak	1 (4.3 oz.)	350	0	30	25	NA	NA	72	4 med. fat meat, 1 fat

☒ = More than 2 fat exchanges per serving   ▲ = More than 800 milligrams sodium   ☕ = High amounts of sugar

Products	SERVING SIZE	CALORIES	CARBO-HYDRATE (gm)	PROTEIN (gm)	FAT (gm)	SAT. FAT (gm)	CHOLES-TEROL (mg)	SODIUM (mg)	Exchanges
Country Style Steak w/Mushroom Sauce	1 (6 oz.)	288	17	18	19	NA	NA	315	1 starch, 2 med. fat meat, 2 fat
Grilled Chicken Breast	1 (5 oz.)	124	2	25	2	NA	NA	500	3 lean meat
Grilled Rainbow Trout	1 (6 oz.)	237	0	34	10	NA	NA	50	4½ lean meat
Sandwiches									
Quarter Pound Hamburger	1 (6.7 oz.)	403	32	25	19	NA	NA	284	2 starch, 3 med. fat meat, 1 fat
Quarter Pound Hamburger w/Cheese	1 (7.2 oz.)	451	32	28	23	NA	NA	432	2 starch, 3½ med. fat meat, 1 fat
Side Items									
Baked Potato w/out Butter	Average (12 oz.)	372	86	8	tr	NA	NA	45	5 starch
Margarine	1 oz.	204	tr	tr	22	NA	NA	268	4½ fat
Green Beans	1 order (4.3 oz.)	40	7	2	1	NA	NA	500	1 vegetable
Broccoli Spears (10 oz.)	1 order	108	14	9	1	NA	NA	30	1 starch or 3 vegetable
Cole Slaw	1 order (2 oz.)	60	4	tr	5	NA	NA	75	1 vegetable, 1 fat
Peppers & Onions	1 order (4.5 oz.)	87	10	1	5	NA	NA	1150	2 vegetable, 1 fat
Mushroom Sauce	1 order (3 oz.)	27	5	1	tr	NA	NA	366	1 vegetable
Barbecue Beans	1 order (7.75 oz.)	296	43	9	13	NA	NA	1100	3 starch, 2 fat
Texas Toast w/out Butter	1 slice (1 oz.)	73	14	2	tr	NA	NA	145	1 starch
Roll	1	158	30	2	4	NA	NA	283	2 starch
Corn Bread	1 piece (2 oz.)	178	28	4	6	NA	NA	263	2 starch, 1 fat
Chili w/Beans	1 order (9 oz.)	346	32	20	16	NA	NA	1380	2 starch, 2 med. fat meat, 1 fat
Vegetable Beef Soup	1 order (8.6 oz.)	78	10	5	2	NA	NA	1046	1 starch

Products	SERVING SIZE	CALORIES	CARBO-HYDRATE (gm)	PROTEIN (gm)	FAT (gm)	SAT. FAT (gm)	CHOLES-TEROL (mg)	SODIUM (mg)	Exchanges
⊟ ⚲ Clam Chowder	1 order (9 oz.)	198	15	6	14	NA	NA	1185	1 starch, 3 fat
⊟ ⚲ Cream of Broccoli Soup	1 order (9 oz.)	193	13	3	14	NA	NA	1045	1 starch, 3 fat

Rally's Hamburgers

Specialties

Products	SERVING SIZE	CALORIES	CARBO-HYDRATE (gm)	PROTEIN (gm)	FAT (gm)	SAT. FAT (gm)	CHOLES-TEROL (mg)	SODIUM (mg)	Exchanges
⊟ ⚲ Rallyburger	1	436	33	21	25	NA	67	955	2 starch, 2 med. fat meat, 3 fat
⊟ ⚲ Rallyburger with Cheese	1	486	33	24	29	NA	79	1185	2 starch, 2½ med. fat meat, 3 fat
⊟ ⚲ Double Cheeseburger	1	733	34	43	49	NA	92	1473	2 starch, 5 med. fat meat, 4 fat
⊟ ⚲ Bacon Cheeseburger	1	622	34	33	40	NA	99	1629	2 starch, 4 med. fat meat, 4 fat
⊟ Chicken Sandwich	1	531	40	18	31	NA	18	364	2½ starch, 2 med. fat meat, 4 fat
Soft Taco	1	223	17	12	10	NA	36	377	1 starch, 2 med. fat meat
⚲ Chili	8 oz.	339	21	22	19	NA	67	1199	1½ starch, 3 med. fat meat
⊟ ⚲ Smokin' Sausage	1 order	724	31	28	55	NA	40	1998	2 starch, 3 med. fat meat, 8 fat
⊟ ⚲ Smokin' Sausage	1 order	830	35	35	62	NA	67	2163	2 starch, 4 med. fat meat, 8 fat

Side Orders

Products	SERVING SIZE	CALORIES	CARBO-HYDRATE (gm)	PROTEIN (gm)	FAT (gm)	SAT. FAT (gm)	CHOLES-TEROL (mg)	SODIUM (mg)	Exchanges
Fries	Regular	158	19	3	8	NA	5	220	1 starch, 2 fat
⊟ Fries	Large	317	39	5	16	NA	10	439	2½ starch, 3 fat

OCCASIONAL USE

Products	SERVING SIZE	CALORIES	CARBO-HYDRATE (gm)	PROTEIN (gm)	FAT (gm)	SAT. FAT (gm)	CHOLES-TEROL (mg)	SODIUM (mg)	Exchanges
♣ Vanilla Shake	1	320	49	10	11	NA	38	197	3 starch, 2 fat
♣ Chocolate Shake	1	411	72	10	12	NA	38	262	4 starch, 2 fat
♣ Strawberry/Banana Shake	1	399	70	10	11	NA	38	223	4 starch, 2 fat

⊟ = More than 2 fat exchanges per serving   ⚲ = More than 800 milligrams sodium   ♣ = High amounts of sugar

Products	SERVING SIZE	CALORIES	CARBO-HYDRATE (gm)	PROTEIN (gm)	FAT (gm)	SAT. FAT (gm)	CHOLES-TEROL (mg)	SODIUM (mg)	Exchanges

RAX

Sandwiches

Products	SERVING SIZE	CALORIES	CARBO-HYDRATE (gm)	PROTEIN (gm)	FAT (gm)	SAT. FAT (gm)	CHOLES-TEROL (mg)	SODIUM (mg)	Exchanges
Regular Rax	1 (4.7 oz.)	262	25	18	10	4	15	707	1½ starch, 2 med. fat meat
Deluxe Roast Beef Sandwich	1 (7.9 oz.)	498	39	21	30	7	36	864	2½ starch, 2 med. fat meat, 3 fat
Beef, Bacon 'n Cheddar	1 (6.7 oz.)	523	37	24	32	8	42	1042	2½ starch, 2½ med. fat meat, 3 fat
Philly Melt	1 (8.2 oz.)	396	40	25	16	7	27	1055	2½ starch, 2½ med. fat meat
Country Fried Chicken Breast Sandwich	1 (7.4 oz.)	618	49	23	29	15	45	1078	3 starch, 3 med. fat meat, 3 fat
Grilled Chicken	1 (6.9 oz.)	402	26	25	23	4	69	872	2 starch, 3 med. fat meat, 1 fat

Side Orders

Products	SERVING SIZE	CALORIES	CARBO-HYDRATE (gm)	PROTEIN (gm)	FAT (gm)	SAT. FAT (gm)	CHOLES-TEROL (mg)	SODIUM (mg)	Exchanges
French Fries	Regular (3.25 oz.)	282	36	3	14	4	3	75	2½ starch, 2 fat
Baked Potato	1 (10 oz.)	264	61	6	0	0	0	15	4 starch
Baked Potato w/Margarine	1 (10.5 oz.) (1 tbsp.)	364	61	6	11	2	0	115	4 starch, 2 fat

Salads

Products	SERVING SIZE	CALORIES	CARBO-HYDRATE (gm)	PROTEIN (gm)	FAT (gm)	SAT. FAT (gm)	CHOLES-TEROL (mg)	SODIUM (mg)	Exchanges
Gourmet Garden Salad without Dressing	1 salad (8.7 oz.)	134	13	7	6	2	2	350	2 vegetable, 1 med. fat meat
with French Dressing	1 (10.7 oz.)	409	33	7	29	5	2	792	2 vegetable, 1 fruit, 1 med. fat meat, 5 fat
with Lite Italian Dressing	1 (10.7 oz.)	196	22	7	10	2	2	643	2 vegetable, ½ fruit, 1 med. fat meat, 1 fat
Grilled Chicken Garden Salad without Dressing	1 (10.7 oz.)	202	14	19	9	2	32	747	2 vegetable, 2 med. fat meat
with French Dressing	1 (12.7 oz.)	477	34	19	31	6	32	1189	2 vegetable, 1 fruit, 2 med. fat meat, 4 fat

Products	SERVING SIZE	CALORIES	CARBO-HYDRATE (gm)	PROTEIN (gm)	FAT (gm)	SAT. FAT (gm)	CHOLES-TEROL (mg)	SODIUM (mg)	Exchanges
☂ with Lite Italian Dressing	(12.7 oz.)	264	22	19	12	3	32	1040	2 vegetable, ½ fruit, 2 med. fat meat

Condiments/Salad Dressings

Products	SERVING SIZE	CALORIES	CARBO-HYDRATE (gm)	PROTEIN (gm)	FAT (gm)	SAT. FAT (gm)	CHOLES-TEROL (mg)	SODIUM (mg)	Exchanges
Mushroom Sauce	1 oz.	16	1	1	tr	0	0	113	Free
Swiss Slice	.4 oz.	42	0	3	3	2	10	157	½ med. fat meat
Barbecue Sauce	1 packet	11	3	0	0	0	0	158	Free
Cheddar Cheese Sauce	1 oz.	29	4	tr	tr	0	2	40	Free
Bacon Slice	.1 oz.	14	0	1	1	tr	2	40	Free
⒝ French Dressing	2 oz.	275	20	0	22	3	0	442	1 fruit, 4 fat
Lite Italian Dressing	2 oz.	63	8	0	3	0	0	294	½ fruit, ½ fat

OCCASIONAL USE

Products	SERVING SIZE	CALORIES	CARBO-HYDRATE (gm)	PROTEIN (gm)	FAT (gm)	SAT. FAT (gm)	CHOLES-TEROL (mg)	SODIUM (mg)	Exchanges
♣ Chocolate Chip Cookies	2 cookies (2 oz.)	262	36	4	12	4	6	192	2 starch, 2 fat

Colombo Yogurt Shakes

Products	SERVING SIZE	CALORIES	CARBO-HYDRATE (gm)	PROTEIN (gm)	FAT (gm)	SAT. FAT (gm)	CHOLES-TEROL (mg)	SODIUM (mg)	Exchanges
♣ Vanilla Fat Free Shakes	10.25 oz.	220	44	9	tr	NA	0	140	3 starch
♣ Chocolate Fat Free Shakes	11.25 oz.	310	66	10	tr	NA	0	180	4 starch
♣ Strawberry Fat Free Shakes	11.25 oz.	300	64	9	tr	NA	0	150	4 starch
♣ Candy Cane Regular Shake	12.10 oz.	320	62	9	4	NA	0	160	4 starch
♣ Cool Orange Regular Shake	12 oz.	360	65	9	4	NA	0	160	4 starch, 1 fat
♣ Peach Regular Shake	12 oz.	320	60	9	4	NA	0	160	4 starch, 1 fat
♣ Blackberry Regular Shake	11.25 oz.	270	58	9	1	NA	0	160	4 starch
♣ Mocha Regular Shake	11.75 oz.	350	64	9	7	NA	7	200	4 starch, 1 fat

NOT RECOMMENDED FOR USE

Products	SERVING SIZE	CALORIES	CARBO-HYDRATE (gm)	PROTEIN (gm)	FAT (gm)	SAT. FAT (gm)	CHOLES-TEROL (mg)	SODIUM (mg)	Exchanges
♣ Chocolate Shake	16 oz.	445	77	9	12	8	35	248	

⒝ = More than 2 fat exchanges per serving   ☂ = More than 800 milligrams sodium   ♣ = High amounts of sugar

Products	SERVING SIZE	CALORIES	CARBO-HYDRATE (gm)	PROTEIN (gm)	FAT (gm)	SAT. FAT (gm)	CHOLES-TEROL (mg)	SODIUM (mg)	Exchanges
Colombo Yogurt Shakes									
Chocolate Chip Regular Shake	11.5 oz.	480	57	10	23	NA	0	150	
Chocolate Covered Cherry Shake	12.5 oz.	540	72	10	23	NA	0	200	
Mint Chocolate Chip Regular Shake	12.5 oz.	570	80	10	23	NA	0	170	
Buckeye/Peanut Butter Kiss Shake	12.5 oz.	660	63	15	41	NA	1	300	

RED LOBSTER

Today's Fresh Catch (All 5 oz. serving size are lunch portions, raw weight. Dinner portion is twice as large.)

Products	SERVING SIZE	CALORIES	CARBO-HYDRATE (gm)	PROTEIN (gm)	FAT (gm)	SAT. FAT (gm)	CHOLES-TEROL (mg)	SODIUM (mg)	Exchanges
Catfish	5 oz.	220	0	20	15	6	99	320	3 med. fat meat
Atlantic Cod	5 oz.	150	0	23	6	3	81	340	3 lean meat
Broiled Flounder Fillets	5 oz.	150	1	21	6	3	80	370	3 lean meat
Grouper	5 oz.	150	0	26	6	3	79	340	3 lean meat
Haddock	5 oz.	160	2	24	6	3	98	450	3 lean meat
Mahi Mahi	5 oz.	160	0	24	6	3	103	125	3 lean meat
Ocean Perch	5 oz.	180	1	24	9	5	87	460	3 lean meat
Yellow Lake Perch	5 oz.	170	1	24	6	3	143	360	3 lean meat
Orange Roughy	5 oz.	220	0	20	15	3	41	360	3 med. fat meat
Red Rock Fish	5 oz.	140	0	21	6	3	96	370	3 lean meat
Atlantic Salmon	5 oz.	230	3	27	17	6	79	330	4 med. fat meat
Coho Salmon	5 oz.	240	3	28	14	5	69	340	4 lean meat
King Salmon	5 oz.	290	3	28	20	4	107	340	4 med. fat meat
Sea Bass	5 oz.	180	1	27	8	4	73	370	4 lean meat
Snapper	5 oz.	160	0	25	6	3	84	410	3 lean meat
Lemon Sole	5 oz.	160	1	27	6	3	75	360	4 lean meat
Swordfish	5 oz.	150	0	17	9	6	298	410	3 lean meat
Rainbow Trout	5 oz.	220	0	23	14	4	105	360	3 med. fat meat
Walleye Pike	5 oz.	170	0	26	6	3	70	55	3 lean meat

Products	SERVING SIZE	CALORIES	CARBO-HYDRATE (gm)	PROTEIN (gm)	FAT (gm)	SAT. FAT (gm)	CHOLES-TEROL (mg)	SODIUM (mg)	Exchanges
Shrimp and Shellfish									
Cherrystone Clams	5 oz.	130	11	18	2	tr	80	540	1 starch, 2 lean meat
✝ Alaskan Snow Crab Legs	16 oz.	200	1	33	11	6	120	1360	5 lean meat
⊟ ✝ Calamari, Breaded & Fried	5 oz.	360	30	13	21	6	140	1150	2 starch, 1 med. fat meat, 3 fat
Oysters	6 raw on half shell	110	11	8	4	2	60	90	1 starch, 1 med. fat meat
Live Maine Lobster	18 oz.	200	5	36	5	2	180	680	5 lean meat
Broiled Rock Lobster	1 tail (13 oz.)	250	2	49	5	2	210	790	7 lean meat
Calico Scallops	5 oz.	180	8	32	2	tr	115	260	½ starch, 4 lean meat
Deep Sea Scallops	5 oz.	130	2	26	2	tr	50	260	3 lean meat
Shrimp	8-12 pieces	120	0	25	2	tr	230	110	3 lean meat
Grilled Shrimp Skewers	20 oz.	290	0	52	9	4	390	120	6 lean meat
Shrimp Scampi	11 Shrimp 1 oz. Sauce	310	0	27	23	14	290	250	4 lean meat 2 fat
✝ Grilled Chicken and Shrimp	4 oz. chicken 10 Shrimp	490	20	55	20	6	300	1830	1 starch, 7 lean meat
✝ Grilled Shrimp Salad with Lite Dressing	3 oz. Shrimp	170	5	20	8	1	300	1240	1 vegetable, 3 lean meat, 1 fat
Other Entrees									
Grilled Chicken Breast	4 oz. lunch	170	0	24	6	2	70	230	3 lean meat
Grilled Chicken Breast	8 oz. dinner	340	0	48	12	4	140	460	6 lean meat
⊟ Porterhouse Steak	18 oz.	1420	0	61	131	55	290	150	8 high fat meat, 13 fat
⊟ Sirloin Steak	7 oz.	570	0	34	48	20	140	85	5 high fat meat, 2 fat

⊟ = More than 2 fat exchanges per serving   ✝ = More than 800 milligrams sodium   ♣ = High amounts of sugar

Products	SERVING SIZE	CALORIES	CARBO-HYDRATE (gm)	PROTEIN (gm)	FAT (gm)	SAT. FAT (gm)	CHOLES-TEROL (mg)	SODIUM (mg)	Exchanges
Strip Streak	7 oz.	690	0	29	64	27	140	70	4 high fat meat, 6 fat
Hamburger	⅓ lb.	320	0	27	23	11	105	70	4 med. fat meat
Accompaniments									
Rice Pilaf	4 oz.	140	28	1	3	tr	0	390	1½ starch, 1 fat
Baked Potato	8 oz.	150	30	3	2	tr	0	410	2 starch
Fresh Vegetables	3 oz.	25	5	2	0	0	0	20	1 vegetable
Appetizers									
Shrimp Cocktail	6 large	90	0	18	2	tr	175	80	2 lean meat
Cocktail Sauce	1 oz.	30	5	2	0	0	0	380	1 vegetable
Bayou-Style Seafood Gumbo	6 oz.	180	24	9	5	1	38	800	1½ starch, 1 med. fat meat
Bayou-Style Seafood Gumbo	12 oz.	350	48	18	9	2	75	1600	3 starch, 2 med. fat meat
FOR OCCASIONAL USE									
Ice Cream	4.5 oz.	260	28	5	14	9	60	110	2 starch, 3 fat
Sherbet	4.5 oz.	180	35	3	3	2	10	60	1 starch, 1 fruit, 1 fat

ROY ROGERS

Sandwiches

Products	SERVING SIZE	CALORIES	CARBO-HYDRATE (gm)	PROTEIN (gm)	FAT (gm)	SAT. FAT (gm)	CHOLES-TEROL (mg)	SODIUM (mg)	Exchanges
Hamburger	1	456	27	24	28	NA	73	495	2 starch, 3 med. fat meat, 2 fat
Small Hamburger	1	222	23	12	9	NA	26	336	1½ starch, 1 med. fat meat, 1 fat
Small Cheeseburger	1	275	24	15	13	NA	36	558	1½ starch, 1½ med. fat meat, 1 fat
Cheeseburger	1	563	27	30	37	NA	95	1404	2 starch, 3½ med. fat meat, 3 fat
RR Bar Burger	1	611	28	36	39	NA	115	1826	2 starch, 4 med. fat meat, 4 fat
Bacon Cheeseburger	1	552	31	32	33	NA	83	1025	2 starch, 4 med. fat meat, 3 fat

Products	SERVING SIZE	CALORIES	CARBO-HYDRATE (gm)	PROTEIN (gm)	FAT (gm)	SAT. FAT (gm)	CHOLES-TEROL (mg)	SODIUM (mg)	Exchanges
⚸ Large Roast Beef Sandwich	1	360	30	34	12	NA	73	1044	2 starch, 4 lean meat
Roast Beef Sandwich	1	317	29	27	10	NA	55	785	2 starch, 3 lean meat
⚸ Large Roast Beef Sandwich w/Cheese	1	427	31	38	17	NA	94	1062	2 starch, 5 lean meat
⊟ ⚸ Fish Sandwich	1	514	58	18	24	NA	62	857	4 starch, 1 med. fat meat, 3 fat
⊟ ⚸ Express Burger	1	561	42	27	32	NA	70	899	3 starch, 3 med. fat meat, 3 fat
⊟ ⚸ Express Cheeseburger	1	613	42	30	37	NA	82	1122	3 starch, 3 med. fat meat, 4 fat
⊟ ⚸ Express Bacon Cheeseburger	1	641	36	33	41	NA	89	1317	2½ starch, 4 med. fat meat, 4 fat
Chicken									
Breast	1	340	15	27	19	NA	104	659	1 starch, 3 med. fat meat, 1 fat
Wing	1	205	9	12	13	NA	48	374	½ starch, 1½ med. fat meat, 1 fat
⚸ Breast & Wing	1	604	25	44	37	NA	165	894	2 starch, 5 med. fat meat, 2 fat
Thigh	1	370	13	20	26	NA	128	489	1 starch, 2 med. fat meat, 3 fat
Leg	1	152	6	12	8	NA	40	207	2 med. fat meat
Thigh & Leg	1	436	17	30	28	NA	125	596	1 starch, 4 med. fat meat, 2 fat
⊟ Chicken Nuggets	6 pieces	288	21	10	18	NA	63	548	1½ starch, 1 med. fat meat, 3 fat
Side Orders									
Biscuit	1	231	26	4	12	NA	<5	575	2 starch, 2 fat
French Fries	4 oz.	268	32	4	12	NA	0	165	2 starch, 2 fat
⊟ Large Fries	5.5 oz.	357	43	5	18	NA	0	221	3 starch, 3 fat
Baked Potato	1 plain	211	48	6	tr	NA	0	65	3 starch

⊟ = More than 2 fat exchanges per serving   ⚸ = More than 800 milligrams sodium   ♥ = High amounts of sugar

Products	SERVING SIZE	CALORIES	CARBO-HYDRATE (gm)	PROTEIN (gm)	FAT (gm)	SAT. FAT (gm)	CHOLES-TEROL (mg)	SODIUM (mg)	Exchanges
with Oleo	1	274	48	6	7	NA	0	161	3 starch, 1 fat
with Sour Cream	1	408	48	7	21	NA	31	138	3 starch, 4 fat
Mashed Potatoes	4 oz.	357	43	5	18	NA	0	221	3 starch, 3 fat
Cole Slaw	1 (4 oz.)	240	13	2	20	NA	10	340	2 vegetable, 4 fat
Salad Bar									
Bacon Bits	1 Tbsp.	33	2	3	1	NA	NA	189	½ fat
Sliced Beets	¼ cup	18	4	tr	tr	NA	NA	162	Free
Broccoli	¼ cup	6	1	1	tr	NA	NA	6	Free
Shredded Carrots	¼ cup	12	3	tr	tr	NA	NA	10	Free
Cheddar Cheese	¼ cup	100	tr	7	8	NA	15	275	1 high fat meat
Chinese Noodles	¼ cup	55	7	2	3	NA	1	113	½ starch, ½ fat
Cucumbers	5-6 slices	4	1	tr	tr	NA	NA	2	Free
Chopped Eggs	2 Tbsp.	55	1	4	4	NA	NA	41	1 med. fat meat
Granola	¼ cup	65	9	2	3	NA	NA	8	½ starch, 1 fat
Green Pepper	2 Tbsp.	3	1	tr	tr	NA	NA	tr	Free
Lettuce	1 cup	7	1	1	tr	NA	NA	4	1 vegetable
Macaroni Salad	¼ cup	93	10	2	5	NA	NA	301	1 starch, 1 fat
Green Peas	¼ cup	28	5	2	tr	NA	NA	41	1 vegetable
Greek Pasta Salad	¼ cup	159	19	3	9	NA	NA	328	1 starch, 2 fat
Potato Salad	¼ cup	54	5	1	3	NA	NA	348	½ starch, 1 fat
Tomatoes	3 slices	20	5	1	tr	NA	NA	3	1 vegetable
Salad Dressings									
Blue Cheese	2 Tbsp.	150	2	2	16	NA	NA	153	3 fat
Bacon n Tomato	2 Tbsp.	136	6	tr	12	NA	NA	150	3 fat
Ranch	2 Tbsp.	155	4	tr	14	NA	NA	100	3 fat
1,000 Island	2 Tbsp.	160	4	tr	16	NA	NA	150	3 fat
Lo-Cal Italian	2 Tbsp.	70	2	tr	6	NA	NA	100	1 fat
Breakfast Items									
Crescent Sandwich	1	408	28	13	27	NA	207	820	2 starch, 1 med. fat meat, 4 fat

Products	SERVING SIZE	CALORIES	CARBO-HYDRATE (gm)	PROTEIN (gm)	FAT (gm)	SAT. FAT (gm)	CHOLES-TEROL (mg)	SODIUM (mg)	Exchanges
Crescent Sandwich w/Bacon	1	446	28	15	30	NA	212	982	2 starch, 1 med. fat meat, 5 fat
Crescent Sandwich w/Sausage	1	564	28	19	42	NA	248	1145	2 starch, 2 med. fat meat, 6 fat
Crescent Sandwich w/Ham	1	456	29	20	29	NA	227	1243	2 starch, 2 med. fat meat, 4 fat
Crescent Roll	1	287	27	5	18	NA	<5	547	2 starch, 3 fat
Rise 'N Shine Biscuit	1	320	34	5	18	NA	0	740	2 starch, 3 fat
Cinnamon 'N Raisin Biscuit	1	320	37	4	17	NA	0	510	2½ starch, 3 fat
Biscuit 'N Gravy	1	440	45	9	24	NA	15	1250	3 starch, 4½ fat
Egg & Biscuit Platter	1	557	44	18	34	NA	417	1020	3 starch, 2 med. fat meat, 4 fat
Egg & Biscuit Platter w/Bacon	1	607	44	21	39	NA	424	1236	3 starch, 2 med. fat meat, 5 fat
Egg & Biscuit Platter w/Ham	1	605	44	21	39	NA	424	1236	3 starch, 2 med. fat meat, 5 fat
Egg & Biscuit Platter w/Sausage	1	713	44	25	49	NA	458	1345	3 starch, 2 med. fat meat, 8 fat
Pancake Platter w/syrup, butter	1	386	63	5	13	NA	51	547	3 starch, 1 fruit, 2 fat
Pancake Platter w/syrup, butter, bacon	1	436	63	8	17	NA	58	763	3 starch, 1 fruit 3 fat
Pancake Platter w/syrup, butter, ham	1	434	64	11	15	NA	71	969	3 starch, 1 fruit 1 med. fat meat, 2 fat
Pancake Platter w/syrup, butter, sausage	1	542	63	11	28	NA	92	872	3 starch, 1 fruit 1 med. fat meat, 4 fat
Hash Rounds	1 order	230	24	3	14	NA	0	560	1½ starch, 3 fat
Cinnamon Roll	1	376	55	5	15	NA	NA	339	3½ starch, 2 fat
Cheese Swirls	1	383	54	8	15	NA	NA	369	3½ starch, 2 fat

⊟ = More than 2 fat exchanges per serving   ⚕ = More than 800 milligrams sodium   ♣ = High amounts of sugar

Products	SERVING SIZE	CALORIES	CARBO-HYDRATE (gm)	PROTEIN (gm)	FAT (gm)	SAT. FAT (gm)	CHOLES-TEROL (mg)	SODIUM (mg)	Exchanges
♥ Apple Swirls	1	328	62	5	7	NA	NA	279	4 starch, 1 fat
Orange Juice	8 oz.	120	32	2	tr	NA	NA	NA	2 fruit
OCCASIONAL USE									
♥ Strawberry Sundae	1	216	33	6	7	NA	23	99	2 starch, 1 fat
♥ Hot Fudge Sundae	1	337	53	7	13	NA	23	186	3½ starch, 2 fat
♥ Caramel Sundae	1	293	52	7	9	NA	23	193	3 starch, 1½ fat
♥ Vanilla Shake	1	306	45	8	11	NA	40	282	3 starch, 2 fat
♥ Chocolate Shake	1	358	61	8	10	NA	37	290	4 starch, 2 fat
♥ Strawberry Shake	1	315	49	8	10	NA	37	261	3 starch, 2 fat
♥ Lemonade	12 oz.	150	39	tr	tr	NA	NA	0	2½ fruit

SHAKEY'S PIZZA RESTAURANT

Thin Crust Pizza

Products	SERVING SIZE	CALORIES	CARBO-HYDRATE (gm)	PROTEIN (gm)	FAT (gm)	SAT. FAT (gm)	CHOLES-TEROL (mg)	SODIUM (mg)	Exchanges
Thin Crust Cheese	one-tenth 12" pizza	133	13	8	5	NA	13	323	1 starch, 1 med. fat meat
Thin Crust Pepperoni	one-tenth 12" pizza	148	13	8	7	NA	14	403	1 starch, 1 med. fat meat
Thin Crust Sausage, Pepperoni	one-tenth 12" pizza	166	13	9	8	NA	17	397	1 starch, 1 high fat meat
Thin Crust Sausage, Mushroom	one-tenth 12" pizza	141	13	9	6	NA	13	336	1 starch, 1 med. fat meat
Thin Crust Onion, Green Pepper, Olive, Mushroom	one-tenth 12" pizza	125	14	7	5	NA	11	313	1 starch, 1 med. fat meat
Thin Crust Shakeys Special	one-tenth 12" pizza	171	14	13	9	NA	16	475	1 starch, 2 med. fat meat

Thick Crust Pizza

Products	SERVING SIZE	CALORIES	CARBO-HYDRATE (gm)	PROTEIN (gm)	FAT (gm)	SAT. FAT (gm)	CHOLES-TEROL (mg)	SODIUM (mg)	Exchanges
Thick Crust Cheese	one-tenth 12" pizza	170	22	9	5	NA	13	421	1½ starch, 1 med. fat meat
Thick Crust Pepperoni	one-tenth 12" pizza	185	22	10	6	NA	17	422	1½ starch, 1 med. fat meat

Products	SERVING SIZE	CALORIES	CARBO-HYDRATE (gm)	PROTEIN (gm)	FAT (gm)	SAT. FAT (gm)	CHOLES-TEROL (mg)	SODIUM (mg)	Exchanges
Thick Crust Sausage, Pepperoni	one-tenth 12" pizza	177	22	11	8	NA	19	424	1½ starch, 1 med. fat meat
Thick Crust Sausage, Mushroom	one-tenth 12" pizza	179	22	10	6	NA	15	420	1½ starch, 1 med. fat meat
Thick Crust Onion, Green Pepper, Mushroom, Olive	one-tenth 12" pizza	162	22	9	4	NA	13	418	1 starch, 1 med. fat meat, 1 vegetable
Thick Shakeys Special	one-tenth 12" pizza	208	22	13	8	NA	18	423	1½ starch, 2 med. fat meat
Homestyle Pizza									
Homestyle Cheese	one-tenth 12" pizza	303	31	14	14	NA	21	591	2 starch, 1½ med. fat meat, 1 fat
Homestyle Onion, Green Peppers, Olives, Mushrooms	one-tenth 12" pizza	320	32	15	14	NA	21	652	2 starch, 1½ med. fat meat, 1 fat
Homestyle Sausage, Pepperoni	one-tenth 12" pizza	374	31	17	20	NA	24	676	2 starch, 2 med. fat meat, 2 fat
Homestyle Sausage, Mushrooms	one-tenth 12" pizza	343	31	16	17	NA	24	677	2 starch, 2 med. fat meat, 1 fat
Homestyle Pepperoni	one-tenth 12" pizza	343	31	16	15	NA	27	740	2 starch, 2 med. fat meat, 1 fat
✝ Homestyle Shakeys Special	one-tenth 12" pizza	384	32	18	21	NA	29	878	2 starch, 2 med. fat meat, 2 fat
Specialties									
⊟ ✝ Shakeys Super Hot Hero	1	810	67	36	44	NA	NA	2688	4½ starch, 3 med. fat meat, 6 fat
✝ Hot Ham & Cheese	1	550	56	36	21	NA	NA	2135	4 starch, 3½ med. fat meat, 1 fat
⊟ ✝ Fried Chicken & Potatoes	3 pieces	947	51	57	56	NA	NA	2293	3½ starch, 6 med. fat meat, 5 fat

⊟ = More than 2 fat exchanges per serving   ✝ = More than 800 milligrams sodium   ☙ = High amounts of sugar

Products	SERVING SIZE	CALORIES	CARBO-HYDRATE (gm)	PROTEIN (gm)	FAT (gm)	SAT. FAT (gm)	CHOLES-TEROL (mg)	SODIUM (mg)	Exchanges
Fried Chicken & Potatoes	5 pieces	1700	130	97	90	NA	NA	5327	8 starch, 10 med. fat meat, 7 fat
Potatoes	15 pieces	950	120	17	36	NA	NA	3703	6 starch, 7 fat
Spaghetti w/Meat Sauce & Garlic Bread	1 order	940	134	26	33	NA	NA	1904	9 starch, 6 fat

SHONEY'S

Entrees

Products	SERVING SIZE	CALORIES	CARBO-HYDRATE (gm)	PROTEIN (gm)	FAT (gm)	SAT. FAT (gm)	CHOLES-TEROL (mg)	SODIUM (mg)	Exchanges
Charbroiled Chicken	1 order	239	1	39	8	NA	85	592	5 lean meat
Hawaiian Chicken	1 order	7	39	8	NA	85	59	593	3 ½ fruit, 5 lean meat
Half O' Pound	1 order	435	0	31	35	NA	123	380	4 med. fat meat, 3 fat
Sirloin	6 oz.	357	0	31	25	NA	99	160	4 med. fat meat 1 fat
Steak N' Shrimp (fried shrimp)	1 order	507	15	37	33	NA	150	249	1 starch, 5 med. fat meat, 1 fat
Steak N' Shrimp	1 order	361	1	37	23	NA	141	198	5 med. fat meat
Ribeye	8 oz.	605	0	35	51	NA	141	211	5 med. fat meat, 5 fat
Country Fried Steak	1 order	449	34	19	27	NA	27	1177	2 starch, 2 med. fat meat, 3 fat
Chicken Tenders	1 order	388	17	35	21	NA	64	239	1 starch, 4 med. fat meat
Lasagna	1 order	297	45	8	10	NA	26	87	3 starch, 2 fat
Spaghetti	1 order	496	63	24	16	NA	55	387	4 starch, 2 med. fat meat, 1 fat
Liver N' Onions	1 order	411	15	35	23	NA	529	321	1 starch, 4½ med. fat meat
Shrimper's Feast	1 order	383	30	17	22	NA	125	216	2 starch, 2 med. fat meat, 2 fat
Shrimper's Feast	Large order	575	45	25	33	NA	188	324	3 starch, 3 med. fat meat, 3 fat
Bite-Size Shrimp	1 order	387	25	16	25	NA	140	1266	1½ starch, 2 fat meat, 3 fat

Products	SERVING SIZE	CALORIES	CARBO-HYDRATE (gm)	PROTEIN (gm)	FAT (gm)	SAT. FAT (gm)	CHOLES-TEROL (mg)	SODIUM (mg)	Exchanges
✝ Baked Fish	1 order	170	2	35	2	NA	83	1641	4 lean meat
✝ Seafood Platter	1 order	566	46	33	28	NA	127	893	3 starch, 3½ med. fat meat, 2 fat
Charbroiled Shrimp	1 order	138	3	25	3	NA	162	170	3 lean meat
Fish N' Shrimp	1 order	487	37	28	26	NA	127	644	2 starch, 3 med. fat meat, 2 fat
▤ ✝ Fish N' Chips (includes fries)	1 order	639	50	32	35	NA	103	873	3 starch, 3 med. fat meat, 4 fat
Light Beef Patty	1 order	289	0	21	23	NA	82	187	3 med. fat meat, 1 fat
Italian Feast	1 order	500	44	38	20	NA	74	369	3 starch, 4 med. fat meat
Boiled Shrimp	1 order	93	0	20	1	NA	182	210	2 lean meat
Light Fried Fish	1 order	297	22	20	14	NA	65	536	1½ starch, 2½ med. fat meat
Shrimp Sampler	1 order	412	26	26	23	NA	217	783	1½ starch, 3 med. fat meat, 1 fat

Sandwiches

Products	SERVING SIZE	CALORIES	CARBO-HYDRATE (gm)	PROTEIN (gm)	FAT (gm)	SAT. FAT (gm)	CHOLES-TEROL (mg)	SODIUM (mg)	Exchanges
▤ All-American Burger	1	501	27	25	33	NA	86	597	2 starch, 3 med. fat meat, 3 fat
Old-Fashioned Burger	1	470	26	25	28	NA	82	681	2 starch, 3 med. fat meat, 2 fat
Chicken Fillet Sandwich	1	464	39	30	21	NA	51	585	2½ starch, 3 med. fat meat, 1 fat
▤ Shoney Burger	1	498	22	23	36	NA	79	782	1½ starch, 3 med. fat meat, 4 fat
✝ Slim Jim Sandwich	1	484	40	27	24	NA	57	1620	2½ starch, 3 med. fat meat, 1 fat
✝ Turkey Club on whole wheat	1	635	44	44	33	NA	100	1289	3 starch, 5 med. med. fat meat, 1 fat
▤ ✝ Ham Club on whole wheat	1	642	45	37	36	NA	78	2105	3 starch, 4 med. fat meat, 3 fat
▤ ✝ Bacon Burger	1	591	29	29	40	NA	86	801	2 starch, 3 med. fat meat, 5 fat

▤ = More than 2 fat exchanges per serving   ✝ = More than 800 milligrams sodium   ☙ = High amounts of sugar

Products	SERVING SIZE	CALORIES	CARBO-HYDRATE (gm)	PROTEIN (gm)	FAT (gm)	SAT. FAT (gm)	CHOLES-TEROL (mg)	SODIUM (mg)	Exchanges
Patty Melt	1	640	30	39	42	NA	121	826	2 starch, 5 med. fat meat, 3 fat
Charbroiled Chicken	1	451	28	43	17	NA	90	1002	2 starch, 5 lean meat
Fish Sandwich	1	323	41	12	13	NA	21	740	2½ starch, 1 med. fat meat, 1 fat
Reuben Sandwich	1	596	32	33	35	NA	138	3873	2 starch, 4 med. fat meat, 3 fat
Philly Steak Sandwich	1	673	37	32	44	NA	103	1242	2½ starch, 4 med. fat meat, 4 fat
Baked Ham Sandwich	1	290	28	19	10	NA	42	1263	2 starch, 2 med. fat meat
Grilled Cheese	1	302	25	12	17	NA	36	880	2 starch, 1 med. fat meat, 2 fat
Grilled Bacon and Cheese	1	440	28	18	28	NA	36	1200	2 starch, 2 med. fat meat, 3 fat
Mushroom/Swiss Burger	1	616	29	32	42	NA	106	1135	2 starch, 4 med. fat meat, 4 fat
Country Fried Sandwich	1	588	67	25	26	NA	29	1501	4 starch, 2 med. fat meat, 3 fat

Side Dishes

Products	SERVING SIZE	CALORIES	CARBO-HYDRATE (gm)	PROTEIN (gm)	FAT (gm)	SAT. FAT (gm)	CHOLES-TEROL (mg)	SODIUM (mg)	Exchanges
Baked Potato	10 oz.	264	61	6	tr	NA	0	16	4 starch
Sauteed Onions	2.5 oz.	37	4	1	2	NA	0	221	1 vegetable
Grecian Bread	1 slice	80	13	2	2	NA	0	94	1 starch
Onion Rings	3	156	15	3	9	NA	6	306	1 starch, 2 fat
Rice	3.5 oz.	137	23	2	4	NA	1	765	1½ starch, 1 fat
Sauteed Mushrooms	3 oz.	75	4	2	7	NA	0	968	1 vegetable, 1 fat
French Fries	3 oz.	189	29	3	8	NA	0	273	2 starch, 1 fat
French Fries	4 oz.	252	39	4	10	NA	0	364	2½ starch, 2 fat

Kid's Menu

Products	SERVING SIZE	CALORIES	CARBO-HYDRATE (gm)	PROTEIN (gm)	FAT (gm)	SAT. FAT (gm)	CHOLES-TEROL (mg)	SODIUM (mg)	Exchanges
Jr. All-American Burger	1	234	20	11	11	NA	30	543	1 starch, 1 med. fat meat, 1 fat
Kid's Chicken Dinner (fried)	1	244	11	22	13	NA	40	151	1 starch, 3 lean meat
Kid's Fried Shrimp	1 order	194	12	8	12	NA	70	633	1 starch, 1 med. fat meat, 1 fat

Products	SERVING SIZE	CALORIES	CARBO-HYDRATE (gm)	PROTEIN (gm)	FAT (gm)	SAT. FAT (gm)	CHOLES-TEROL (mg)	SODIUM (mg)	Exchanges
Kid's Spaghetti	1 order	247	32	12	8	NA	27	193	2 starch, 1 med. fat meat
Kid's Fish N' Chips	1 order	337	33	14	17	NA	41	467	2 starch, 1 med. fat meat, 2 fat

Soups

Products	SERVING SIZE	CALORIES	CARBO-HYDRATE (gm)	PROTEIN (gm)	FAT (gm)	SAT. FAT (gm)	CHOLES-TEROL (mg)	SODIUM (mg)	Exchanges
Tomato Vegetable	6 oz.	46	10	2	tr	NA	0	314	2 vegetable
Chicken Rice	6 oz.	72	13	3	tr	NA	6	117	1 starch
Tomato Florentine	6 oz.	63	11	2	1	NA	0	683	1 starch
Bean	6 oz.	63	10	4	1	NA	4	479	1 starch
Cream of Chicken Vegetable	6 oz.	79	13	4	1	NA	NA	714	1 starch
Chicken Noodle	6 oz.	62	10	3	1	NA	14	127	1 starch
⋏ Vegetable Beef	6 oz.	82	14	4	1	NA	5	1254	1 starch
⋏ Cheddar Chowder	6 oz.	91	14	3	2	NA	NA	948	1 starch
Beef Cabbage	6 oz.	86	9	6	3	NA	13	503	1 starch
Potato	6 oz.	102	17	1	4	NA	0	335	1 starch, 1 fat
Corn Chowder	6 oz.	148	22	4	5	NA	NA	510	1½ starch, 1 fat
⋏ Cream of Chicken	6 oz.	136	14	5	9	NA	11	1164	1 starch, 2 fat

Salad Bar

Products	SERVING SIZE	CALORIES	CARBO-HYDRATE (gm)	PROTEIN (gm)	FAT (gm)	SAT. FAT (gm)	CHOLES-TEROL (mg)	SODIUM (mg)	Exchanges
Lettuce	1.8 oz.	7	1	1	tr	NA	0	5	Free
Spinach	¼ cup	1	tr	tr	0	NA	0	4	Free
Broccoli	¼ cup	4	1	0	tr	NA	0	4	Free
Carrot	¼ cup	10	2	tr	tr	NA	0	8	Free
Cauliflower	¼ cup	8	2	1	tr	NA	0	5	Free
Olives	2	10	0	0	1	NA	0	38	Free
Prunes	1 tbsp.	19	5	tr	0	NA	0	0	Free
Apple Ring	1	15	4	0	0	NA	0	3	Free
Pineapple Bits	1 tbsp.	9	2	tr	0	NA	0	2	Free
Grapefruit	¼ cup	24	6	tr	tr	NA	0	5	½ fruit
Wheat Bread	1 slice	71	14	3	1	NA	0	150	1 starch

🖩 = More than 2 fat exchanges per serving   ⋏ = More than 800 milligrams sodium   🍬 = High amounts of sugar

Products	SERVING SIZE	CALORIES	CARBO-HYDRATE (gm)	PROTEIN (gm)	FAT (gm)	SAT. FAT (gm)	CHOLES-TEROL (mg)	SODIUM (mg)	Exchanges
Bacon Bits	1 spoon	15	1	1	tr	NA	NA	NA	Free
Chow Mein	1 spoon	13	tr	tr	1	NA	0	0	Free
Sunflower Seeds	1 spoon	40	1	2	3	NA	0	2	1 fat
Croutons	1 spoon	13	2	tr	tr	NA	0	38	Free
Raisins	1 spoon	26	7	tr	0	NA	0	1	½ fruit
Whipped Margarine	2 tsp.	46	0	0	5	NA	0	32	1 fat
Melba Toast	8	80	16	4	0	NA	0	180	1 starch
Turkey Ham	2 Tbsp.	24	tr	4	1	NA	2	242	½ lean meat
Pepperoni	2 Tbsp.	60	0	5	5	NA	NA	162	1 med. fat meat
Diced Egg	2 Tbsp.	30	tr	3	2	NA	108	28	½ med. fat meat
Shredded Cheese	2 Tbsp.	42	1	3	3	NA	4	224	½ med. fat meat
Cottage Cheese	2 Tbsp.	24	1	4	tr	NA	2	132	½ lean meat

Salad Dressings

Products	SERVING SIZE	CALORIES	CARBO-HYDRATE (gm)	PROTEIN (gm)	FAT (gm)	SAT. FAT (gm)	CHOLES-TEROL (mg)	SODIUM (mg)	Exchanges
W. W. Italian	2 Tbsp.	10	2	0	0	NA	0	615	Free
Blue Cheese	2 Tbsp.	113	0	0	13	NA	15	109	2 fat
Thousand Island	2 Tbsp.	130	2	1	13	NA	12	179	3 fat
Ranch	2 Tbsp.	95	0	0	10	NA	15	10	2 fat
French	2 Tbsp.	124	2	2	12	NA	12	204	3 fat
Rue French	2 Tbsp.	122	2	5	10	NA	0	364	2 fat
Creamy Italian	2 Tbsp.	135	1	0	15	NA	0	454	3 fat
Golden Italian	2 Tbsp.	141	1	0	15	NA	0	302	3 fat
Honey Mustard	2 Tbsp.	165	2	2	17	NA	18	5	3 fat

Prepared Salads

Products	SERVING SIZE	CALORIES	CARBO-HYDRATE (gm)	PROTEIN (gm)	FAT (gm)	SAT. FAT (gm)	CHOLES-TEROL (mg)	SODIUM (mg)	Exchanges	
Mixed Fruit	¼ cup	37	9	tr	tr	NA	0	3	½ fruit	
Jello	¼ cup	40	9	1	0	NA	0	2	6	½ fruit
JelloFluff	¼ cup	16	3	tr	tr	NA	0	0	Free	
Macaroni Salad	¼ cup	207	17	4	14	NA	14	382	1 starch, 3 fat	
Cucumber Lite	¼ cup	12	3	tr	tr	NA	0	344	Free	
Cole Slaw	¼ cup	69	5	1	5	NA	7	106	1 vegetable, 1 fat	
Three Bean Salad	¼ cup	96	12	2	5	NA	0	189	1 starch, 1 fat	

Products	SERVING SIZE	CALORIES	CARBO-HYDRATE (gm)	PROTEIN (gm)	FAT (gm)	SAT. FAT (gm)	CHOLES-TEROL (mg)	SODIUM (mg)	Exchanges
Pea Salad	¼ cup	60	4	2	6	NA	42	89	1 vegetable, 1 fat
Broccoli & Cauliflower	¼ cup	98	4	2	9	NA	0	478	1 vegetable, 2 fat
Rotelli Pasta	¼ cup	78	9	1	4	NA	0	82	½ starch, 1 fat
Don's Pasta	¼ cup	82	9	2	5	NA	0	223	½ starch, 1 fat
Spaghetti Salad	¼ cup	81	9	2	5	NA	0	20	½ starch, 1 fat
Ambrosia Salad	¼ cup	75	12	tr	3	NA	0	167	1 fruit
Mixed Squash	¼ cup	49	2	1	4	NA	0	230	1 fat
Oriental Salad	¼ cup	79	13	1	3	NA	1	31	1 starch
Carrot Apple	¼ cup	99	4	1	9	NA	8	10	2 fat
Beet Onion Salad	¼ cup	25	3	1	1	NA	0	167	Free
Kidney Bean Salad	¼ cup	55	7	3	2	NA	2	154	½ starch
Waldorf	¼ cup	81	9	1	5	NA	2	68	½ fruit, 1 fat
Chocolate Pudding	¼ cup	81	16	2	2	NA	7	81	1 starch

Breakfast Items

Products	SERVING SIZE	CALORIES	CARBO-HYDRATE (gm)	PROTEIN (gm)	FAT (gm)	SAT. FAT (gm)	CHOLES-TEROL (mg)	SODIUM (mg)	Exchanges
Pancakes	1 (6" cake)	91	20	2	tr	NA	0	522	1 starch
Biscuit	1	170	22	3	8	NA	0	364	1½ starch, 1 fat
Hashbrowns	3 oz.	90	14	2	3	NA	0	50	1 starch
Grits	3 oz.	57	6	1	3	NA	0	62	½ starch
Buttered Toast	2 slices	163	25	4	5	NA	0	296	2 starch, 1 fat
Bacon Strip	3	109	tr	6	9	NA	16	303	1 high fat meat
Egg, fried	1	159	tr	6	15	NA	274	69	1 med. fat meat, 2 fat
Sirloin Steak, charbroiled	6 oz.	357	0	32	25	NA	99	160	5 med. fat meat
Home Fries	3 oz.	115	18	2	4	NA	0	53	1 starch, 1 fat
Sausage Patty	1	103	tr	4	10	NA	17	161	2 fat
Breakfast Ham	2 slices	59	1	7	2	NA	28	526	1 lean meat
Blueberry Muffin	2	214	35	3	7	NA	33	2	2 starch, 1 fat
Low-Cal Syrup	2.2 oz.	98	24	0	0	NA	0	0	1½ fruit
Country Gravy	3 oz.	114	6	1	10	NA	2	358	2 fat
Honey Bun	1	265	32	4	14	NA	3	33	2 starch, 3 fat

B = More than 2 fat exchanges per serving   ▲ = More than 800 milligrams sodium   ♥ = High amounts of sugar

Products	SERVING SIZE	CALORIES	CARBO-HYDRATE (gm)	PROTEIN (gm)	FAT (gm)	SAT. FAT (gm)	CHOLES-TEROL (mg)	SODIUM (mg)	Exchanges
Croissant	1	260	22	5	16	NA	2	260	1½ starch, 3 fat
English Muffin	1	140	27	4	2	NA	0	280	2 starch
Orange Juice	4 oz.	54	13	0	tr	NA	0	1	1 fruit
Tomato Juice	4 oz.	24	5	1	tr	NA	0	251	1 vegetable
Margarine	.75 oz.	153	tr	tr	17	NA	0	201	3 fat

OCCASIONAL USE

Products	SERVING SIZE	CALORIES	CARBO-HYDRATE (gm)	PROTEIN (gm)	FAT (gm)	SAT. FAT (gm)	CHOLES-TEROL (mg)	SODIUM (mg)	Exchanges
Strawberry Pie	1 piece	332	45	2	17	NA	0	247	2 starch, 1 fruit 3 fat
Hot Fudge Sundae	1	451	48	6	19	NA	60	226	3 starch, 4 fat
Strawberry Sundae	1	380	48	6	19	NA	69	145	3 starch, 4 fat

NOT RECOMMENDED FOR USE

Products	SERVING SIZE	CALORIES	CARBO-HYDRATE (gm)	PROTEIN (gm)	FAT (gm)	SAT. FAT (gm)	CHOLES-TEROL (mg)	SODIUM (mg)	Exchanges
Hot Fudge Cake	1 piece	522	82	7	20	NA	27	485	
Apple Pie A la Mode	1 slice	492	67	6	23	NA	35	574	
Carrot Cake	1 piece	500	56	9	26	NA	37	476	
Walnut Brownie A La Mode	1 serving	576	61	10	34	NA	35	435	

SKIPPER'S

Thick Cut Cod

Products	SERVING SIZE	CALORIES	CARBO-HYDRATE (gm)	PROTEIN (gm)	FAT (gm)	SAT. FAT (gm)	CHOLES-TEROL (mg)	SODIUM (mg)	Exchanges
3 piece, fries	1 meal	665	68	27	32	NA	38	1054	4 starch, 2 med. fat meat, 4 fat
4 piece, fries	1 meal	759	74	34	36	NA	50	1388	5 starch, 3 med. fat meat, 3 fat
5 piece, fries	1 meal	853	80	42	41	NA	62	1723	5 starch, 4 med. fat meat, 4 fat

Famous Fish Fillets

Products	SERVING SIZE	CALORIES	CARBO-HYDRATE (gm)	PROTEIN (gm)	FAT (gm)	SAT. FAT (gm)	CHOLES-TEROL (mg)	SODIUM (mg)	Exchanges
1 fish, fries	1 meal	558	51	17	28	NA	55	408	3½ starch, 1½ med. fat meat, 4 fat

Products	SERVING SIZE	CALORIES	CARBO-HYDRATE (gm)	PROTEIN (gm)	FAT (gm)	SAT. FAT (gm)	CHOLES-TEROL (mg)	SODIUM (mg)	Exchanges
🭱 2 fish, fries	1 meal	733	71	28	38	NA	108	765	4½ starch, 3 med. fat meat, 4 fat
🭱 ⌁ 3 fish, fries	1 meal	908	82	39	48	NA	160	1122	5½ starch, 4 med. fat meat, 4 fat
Seafood Combos									
🭱 ⌁ Jumbo shrimp, 1 fish, fries	1 meal	720	75	24	36	NA	91	1268	5 starch, 2 med. fat meat, 4 fat
🭱 ⌁ Original shrimp, 1 fish, fries	1 meal	728	77	24	37	NA	105	943	5 starch, 2 med. fat meat, 4 fat
🭱 Clam strips, 1 fish, fries	1 meal	868	81	25	54	NA	61	667	5 starch, 2 med. fat meat, 7 fat
🭱 ⌁ Oysters, 1 fish, fries	1 meal	885	95	25	44	NA	80	809	6 starch, 2 med. fat meat, 6 fat
Seafood Baskets									
🭱 ⌁ Jumbo shrimp, fries	1	707	79	20	35	NA	73	911	5 starch, 1 med. fat meat, 5 fat
🭱 ⌁ Original shrimp, fries	1	723	82	20	36	NA	102	1121	5 starch, 2 med. fat meat, 4 fat
🭱 Clam strips, fries	1	1003	90	22	70	NA	14	569	6 starch, 2 med. fat meat, 9 fat
🭱 ⌁ Oysters, fries	1	1038	118	28	51	NA	52	853	7 starch, 2 med. fat meat, 7 fat
🭱 ⌁ Skipper's Platter, fries	1	1038	97	32	63	NA	111	1202	6 starch, 3 med. fat meat, 8 fat
Chicken Tenderloin Strips									
🭱 5 piece, fries	1 meal	793	69	44	38	NA	77	798	4½ starch, 4 med. fat meat, 3 fat
🭱 ⌁ 3 piece, 1 fish, fries	1 meal	805	72	40	40	NA	100	858	5 starch, 4 med. fat meat, 3 fat
🭱 ⌁ 3 piece, Original shrimp, fries	1 meal	800	77	36	39	NA	97	1036	5 starch, 3 med. fat meat, 4 fat
Salads & Lite Catch									
⌁ 2 fish, small green salad	1 meal	409	27	25	23	NA	119	937	1 starch, 2 vegetable, 3 med. fat meat, 1 fat

🭱 = More than 2 fat exchanges per serving   ⌁ = More than 800 milligrams sodium   ❀ = High amounts of sugar

Products	SERVING SIZE	CALORIES	CARBO-HYDRATE (gm)	PROTEIN (gm)	FAT (gm)	SAT. FAT (gm)	CHOLES-TEROL (mg)	SODIUM (mg)	Exchanges
3 chicken, small green salad	1 meal	305	17	26	15	NA	58	673	1 starch, 1 vegetable, 3 med. fat meat
1 fish, 2 chicken, small green salad	1 meal	399	24	29	21	NA	96	880	1 starch, 2 vegetable, 3 med. fat meat, 1 fat

Sandwiches

Fish sandwich	1	524	43	19	33	NA	86	1191	3 starch, 1½ med. fat meat, 4 fat
Double Fish sandwich	1	698	54	30	43	NA	139	1548	3½ starch, 3 med. fat meat, 5 fat
Chicken sandwich	1	606	44	31	32	NA	82	976	3 starch, 3 med. fat meat, 3 fat

Side Orders

Chicken strip	1 order	82	4	8	4	NA	15	150	I med. fat meat
Fish fillet	1 order	175	11	11	10	NA	53	357	1 starch, 1 med. fat meat, 1 fat
Fries	1 order	383	50	6	18	NA	2	51	3 starch, 3 fat
Clam chowder	1 cup	100	14	3	4	NA	12	525	1 starch, 1 fat
Coleslaw	5 oz.	289	10	2	27	NA	50	329	2 vegetable, 5 fat
Small green salad	1	59	6	3	3	NA	13	223	1 vegetable, 1 fat
Shrimp and seafood salad	1	167	15	23	3	NA	80	657	1 vegetable, 3 lean meat

Salad Dressings

1000 Island	1 pouch	160	8	0	14	NA	6	415	½ starch, 3 fat
Blue Cheese	1 pouch	222	4	1	23	NA	8	240	5 fat
Gourmet Italian	1 pouch	140	2	0	15	NA	0	200	3 fat
Lo-cal Italian	1 pouch	17	2	0	1	NA	0	680	Free
Ranch House	1 pouch	188	2	1	20	NA	0	302	4 fat

Condiments

Barbeque Sauce	1 Tbsp.	25	5	0	1	NA	0	226	Free
Cocktail Sauce	1 Tbsp.	20	5	0	0	NA	0	216	Free
Tartar Sauce	1 Tbsp.	65	0	0	7	NA	4	102	1 fat

Products	SERVING SIZE	CALORIES	CARBO-HYDRATE (gm)	PROTEIN (gm)	FAT (gm)	SAT. FAT (gm)	CHOLES-TEROL (mg)	SODIUM (mg)	Exchanges

SUBWAY

Subs

Products	SERVING SIZE	CALORIES	CARBO-HYDRATE (gm)	PROTEIN (gm)	FAT (gm)	SAT. FAT (gm)	CHOLES-TEROL (mg)	SODIUM (mg)	Exchanges
Cold Cut Comb Sub	6 inch	427	41	23	20	6	80	1110	3 starch, 2 med. fat meat, 1 fat
Spicy Italian Sub	6 inch	522	41	21	32	12	70	1510	3 starch, 2 med. fat meat, 3 fat
BMT Sub	6 inch	491	41	22	28	10	70	1570	3 starch, 2 med. fat meat, 3 fat
Subway Club Sub	6 inch	346	42	23	11	4	40	1360	3 starch, 2 med. fat meat
Tuna Sub	6 inch	552	41	18	36	7	40	750	3 starch, 2 med. fat meat, 4 fat
Seafood & Crab Sub	6 inch	493	47	15	28	6	30	980	3 starch, 2 med. fat meat, 3 fat
Seafood & Lobster Sub	6 inch	472	47	14	26	5	30	1040	3 starch, 2 med. fat meat, 2 fat
Meatball Sub	6 inch	458	48	21	22	8	40	1010	3 starch, 2 med. fat meat, 2 fat
Steak & Cheese Sub	6 inch	383	42	22	16	6	40	790	3 starch, 2 med. fat meat
Turkey Breast Sub	6 inch	322	41	20	10	3	30	1230	3 starch, 2 lean meat
Roast Beef Sub	6 inch	345	42	21	12	4	40	1140	3 starch, 2 lean meat
Ham & Cheese Sub	6 inch	322	41	19	9	3	40	1220	3 starch, 2 lean meat
Veggies & Cheese Sub	6 inch	268	41	10	9	3	10	540	3 starch, ½ med. fat meat

Salads/Salad Dressings

Products	SERVING SIZE	CALORIES	CARBO-HYDRATE (gm)	PROTEIN (gm)	FAT (gm)	SAT. FAT (gm)	CHOLES-TEROL (mg)	SODIUM (mg)	Exchanges
Cold Cut Combo Salad	Small	305	12	18	25	6	80	910	2 vegetable, 2 med. fat meat, 3 fat
Cold Cut Combo Salad	Regular	506	14	33	37	11	170	1820	2 vegetable, 4 med. fat meat, 4 fat
Spicy Italian Salad	Small	400	12	16	33	12	70	1140	2 vegetable, 2 med. fat meat, 5 fat

〇 = More than 2 fat exchanges per serving   ☀ = More than 800 milligrams sodium   ✿ = High amounts of sugar

Products	SERVING SIZE	CALORIES	CARBO-HYDRATE (gm)	PROTEIN (gm)	FAT (gm)	SAT. FAT (gm)	CHOLES-TEROL (mg)	SODIUM (mg)	Exchanges
Spicy Italian Salad	Regular	696	14	29	60	22	140	2280	2 vegetable, 4 med. fat meat, 8 fat
BMT Salad	Small	369	12	17	29	10	70	1200	2 vegetable, 2 med. fat meat, 4 fat
BMT Salad	Regular	635	14	31	52	23	130	2400	2 vegetable, 4 med. fat meat, 6 fat
Subway Club Salad	Small	225	12	18	13	3	40	990	2 vegetable, 2 med. fat meat, 1 fat
Subway Club Salad	Regular	346	14	32	19	6	80	1980	2 vegetable, 4 med. fat meat
Tuna Salad	Small	430	12	13	38	6	40	380	2 vegetable, 2 med. fat meat, 5 fat
Tuna Salad	Regular	756	12	23	68	12	90	760	2 vegetable, 3 med. fat meat, 10 fat
Seafood & Crab Salad	Small	371	18	10	30	5	30	610	2 vegetable, 1 med. fat meat, 5 fat
Seafood & Crab Salad	Regular	639	25	16	53	10	60	1230	2 vegetable, 1 starch, 2 med. fat meat, 8 fat
Seafood & Lobster Salad	Small	351	18	9	28	5	30	670	2 vegetable, 1 med. fat meat, 5 fat
Seafood & Lobster Salad	Regular	597	26	15	49	9	60	1340	2 vegetable, 1 starch, 2 med. fat meat, 7 fat
Turkey Breast Salad	Small	201	12	15	11	3	30	860	2 vegetable, 2 med. fat meat
Turkey Breast Salad	Regular	297	14	27	16	5	70	1720	2 vegetable, 3 med. fat meat
Roast Beef Salad	Small	222	13	16	10	4	40	780	2 vegetable, 2 med. fat meat
Roast Beef Salad	Regular	340	15	29	20	7	80	1550	2 vegetable, 4 med. fat meat
Ham & Cheese Salad	Small	200	11	14	12	3	40	860	2 vegetable, 2 med. fat meat
Ham & Cheese Salad	Regular	296	12	25	18	6	70	1710	2 vegetable, 3 med. fat meat, 1 fat
Veggies & Cheese Salad	Regular	188	12	7	14	4	20	340	2 vegetable, ½ med. fat meat, 2 fat

Products	SERVING SIZE	CALORIES	CARBO-HYDRATE (gm)	PROTEIN (gm)	FAT (gm)	SAT. FAT (gm)	CHOLES-TEROL (mg)	SODIUM (mg)	Exchanges
⌷ Blue Cheese	2 oz.	322	14	2	29	5	274	578	1 starch, 6 fat
⌷ Thousand Island	2 oz.	252	10	1	24	4	186	514	½ starch, 5 fat
⌷ Lite-Italian	2 oz.	23	4	1	1	tr	10	952	Free
⌷ French	2 oz.	264	20	tr	20	3	1	462	1 starch, 4 fat
⌷ Creamy Italian	2 oz.	256	5	tr	26	4	119	548	5 fat

TACO BELL

Specialties

8 Bean Burrito	1 (6.7 OZ.)	359	54	13	11	5	13	922	3½ starch, 1 med. fat meat, 1 fat
☥ Beef Burrito	1 (6.7 OZ.)	402	38	22	17	8	59	993	2½ starch, 2 med. fat meat, 1 fat
☥ Double Beef Burrito Supreme	1 (9 OZ.)	451	40	23	22	10	59	928	3 starch, 2 med. fat meat, 2 fat
Tostada	1 (5.5 OZ.)	243	28	10	11	5	18	670	2 starch, 1 med. fat meat, 1 fat
Beefy Tostada	1 (7 OZ.)	322	22	15	20	10	40	764	1½ starch, 1½ med. fat meat, 2 fat
Beef Meximelt	1 (3.7 oz.)	266	19	13	15	8	38	689	1 starch, 1½ med. fat meat, 2 fat
Chicken Meximelt	1 (3.8 oz.)	257	19	14	15	7	48	779	1 starch, 1½ med. fat meat, 2 fat
☥ Bellbeefer	1 (6.2 oz.)	312	32	16	13	6	39	855	2 starch, 1½ med. fat meat, 1 fat
☥ Chicken Burrito	1 (6 oz.)	334	38	17	12	4	52	880	2½ starch, 2 med. fat meat
☥ Burrito Supreme	1 (8.7 oz.)	422	46	17	19	9	35	952	3 starch, 1½ med. fat meat, 2 fat
☥ Combination Burrito	1 (6.7 oz.)	380	46	17	14	6	36	957	3 starch, 1½ med. fat meat, 1 fat
☥ Enchirito	1 (7.5 oz.)	382	30	21	20	10	56	1260	2 starch, 2 med. fat meat, 2 fat
Taco	1 (2.75 oz.)	184	11	10	11	4	32	274	1 starch, 2 lean meat

⌷ = More than 2 fat exchanges per serving   ☥ = More than 800 milligrams sodium   ❀ = High amounts of sugar

Products	SERVING SIZE	CALORIES	CARBO-HYDRATE (gm)	PROTEIN (gm)	FAT (gm)	SAT. FAT (gm)	CHOLES-TEROL (mg)	SODIUM (mg)	Exchanges
Chicken Soft Taco	1 (3.7 oz.)	213	19	14	10	4	52	615	1 starch, 2 med. fat meat
Taco Light Platter	1 (17 oz.)	1062	97	38	58	34	82	2068	6 starch, 3 med. fat meat, 8 fat
Burrito Supreme Platter	1 (16 oz.)	774	76	35	37	19	79	1920	5 starch, 3 med. meat, 4 fat
Cheesarito	1 (4 oz.)	312	37	12	13	7	29	451	2 starch, 1 med. meat, 2 fat
Mexican Pizza	1 (9.5 oz.)	714	43	28	48	31	81	1364	3 starch, 3 med. fat meat, 6 fat
Taco Bellgrande Platter	1 (17 oz.)	1002	99	37	51	29	80	1962	6½ starch, 3 med. fat meat, 6 fat
Pintos & Cheese	1 order (4.5 oz.)	194	19	9	10	5	19	733	1 starch, 1 med. fat meat, 1 fat
Nachos	1 order (3.7 oz.)	346	37	7	18	6	9	399	2½ starch, 4 fat
Nachos Bellgrande	1 order (10 oz.)	649	61	22	35	12	36	997	4 starch, 2 med. fat meat, 6 fat
Taco Bellgrande	1 (6 oz.)	351	20	18	22	13	55	470	1 starch, 2 med. fat meat, 3 fat
Taco Light	1 (6 oz.)	411	18	19	29	18	57	575	1 starch, 2 med. fat meat, 4 fat
Soft Taco	1 (3.25 oz.)	228	18	12	12	5	32	516	1 starch, 1½ med. fat meat, 1 fat
Fajita Steak Taco	1 (5 oz.)	235	20	15	11	5	14	507	1 starch, 2 med. fat meat
Fajita Steak Taco w/Sour Cream	1 (5.75 oz.)	281	21	15	15	7	14	507	1 starch, 2 med. fat meat, 1 fat
Fajita Steak Taco w/Guacamole	1 (5.75 oz.)	269	23	15	13	5	14	620	1 starch, 2 med. fat meat, 1 fat
Chicken Fajita	1 (4.75 oz.)	226	20	14	10	4	44	619	1 starch, 2 med. fat meat
Cinnamon Crisps	1 order (1.6 oz.)	266	20	3	16	13	2	122	2 starch, 3 fat

Condiments

Taco Sauce	1 packet	2	tr	tr	tr	0	0	126	Free

Products	SERVING SIZE	CALORIES	CARBO-HYDRATE (gm)	PROTEIN (gm)	FAT (gm)	SAT. FAT (gm)	CHOLES-TEROL (mg)	SODIUM (mg)	Exchanges
Salsa	1 packet (.35 oz.)	18	4	1	tr	0	0	376	Free
▯ Ranch Dressing	1 packet (2.6 oz.)	236	1	2	25	5	35	571	5 fat
Guacamole	1 serving (.75 oz.)	34	3	tr	2	tr	0	113	½ fat

Salads

Products	SERVING SIZE	CALORIES	CARBO-HYDRATE (gm)	PROTEIN (gm)	FAT (gm)	SAT. FAT (gm)	CHOLES-TEROL (mg)	SODIUM (mg)	Exchanges
▯ ⵣ Taco Salad w/out Beans	1 (18 oz.)	822	47	31	57	38	81	1368	3 starch, 3 med. fat meat, 8 fat
▯ ⵣ Taco Salad w/out Salsa	1 (18 oz.)	931	60	35	62	40	85	1387	4 starch, 3½ med. fat meat, 8 fat
▯ ⵣ Taco Salad with Ranch Dressing	1 (20 oz.)	1167	61	37	87	45	121	1959	4 starch, 3½ med. fat meat, 13 fat
▯ ⵣ Seafood Salad w/Ranch Dressing	1 (15 oz.)	884	49	25	66	34	117	1489	3 starch, 3 med. fat meat, 10 fat
Seafood Salad w/out Dressing/ Shell	1 (10 oz.)	217	12	18	11	6	81	693	1 starch, 2 med. fat meat
▯ ⵣ Seafood Salad w/out Dressing	1 (13 oz.)	648	47	24	42	30	82	917	3 starch, 2 med. fat meat, 6 fat
▯ ⵣ Taco Salad w/Salsa	1 (21 oz.)	949	63	36	62	40	86	1763	4 starch, 4 med. fat meat, 8 fat
▯ ⵣ Taco Salad w/out Shell	1 (18.7 oz.)	502	26	29	31	14	80	1056	2 starch, 3 med. fat meat, 3 fat
ⵣ Taco Salad w/Salsa, w/out Shell	1 (18.7 oz.)	520	30	31	31	14	80	1431	2 starch, 4 med. fat meat, 2 fat

TCBY (YOGURT)

Regular

Products	SERVING SIZE	CALORIES	CARBO-HYDRATE (gm)	PROTEIN (gm)	FAT (gm)	SAT. FAT (gm)	CHOLES-TEROL (mg)	SODIUM (mg)	Exchanges
TCBY	Kiddie (3.2 oz.)	104	18	3	2	2	8	48	1 starch
TCBY	Small (5.9 oz.)	192	34	6	4	3	15	88	2 starch

▯ = More than 2 fat exchanges per serving   ⵣ = More than 800 milligrams sodium   ☀ = High amounts of sugar

Products	SERVING SIZE	CALORIES	CARBO-HYDRATE (gm)	PROTEIN (gm)	FAT (gm)	SAT. FAT (gm)	CHOLES-TEROL (mg)	SODIUM (mg)	Exchanges
TCBY	Regular (8.2 oz.)	266	47	6	6	4	20	123	3 starch, 1 fat
TCBY	Large (10.5 oz.)	341	60	10	8	5	26	158	4 starch, 1 fat
Nonfat									
TCBY	Kiddie (3.2 oz.)	88	18	3	tr	tr	tr	36	1 starch
TCBY	Small (5.9 oz.)	162	34	6	tr	tr	tr	66	2 starch
TCBY	Regular (8.2 oz.)	226	47	8	tr	tr	tr	92	3 starch
TCBY	Large (10.5 oz.)	289	60	10	tr	tr	tr	118	4 starch
Sugar Free									
TCBY	Kiddie (3.2 oz.)	64	15	3	tr	tr	tr	32	1 starch
TCBY	Small (5.9 oz.)	118	27	6	tr	tr	tr	59	1½ starch
TCBY	Regular (8.2 oz.)	164	37	8	tr	tr	tr	82	2½ starch
TCBY	Large (10.5 oz.)	210	47	10	tr	tr	tr	105	3 starch

WENDY'S

Sandwiches

Single Hamburger on Bun	1 (4.7 oz.)	350	31	25	15	6	70	510	2 starch, 3 med. fat meat
☀ Single with Everything	1 (7.7 oz.)	440	36	26	23	7	75	850	2 starch, 1 vegetable 3 med. fat meat, 1 fat
Double Hamburger on bun	1 (7 oz.)	560	26	44	30	11	150	465	2 starch, 6 med. fat meat
☀ Big Classic on Kaiser Bun	1 (8.9 oz.)	480	44	27	23	7	75	850	3 starch, 3 med. fat meat, 1 fat
Double w/Cheese	1 (7.8 oz.)	620	26	48	36	15	165	760	2 starch, 6 med. fat meat, 1 fat

Products	SERVING SIZE	CALORIES	CARBO-HYDRATE (gm)	PROTEIN (gm)	FAT (gm)	SAT. FAT (gm)	CHOLES-TEROL (mg)	SODIUM (mg)	Exchanges
Bacon Cheeseburger	1 (5.3 oz.)	440	26	30	24	20	95	680	2 starch, 3 med. fat meat, 2 fat
🅱🌡 Country Fried Steak	1 (5.4 oz.)	460	45	15	26	7	35	880	3 starch, 1 med. fat meat, 4 fat
Fish Sandwich	1 (6.4 oz.)	460	42	18	25	5	55	780	3 starch, 2 med. fat meat, 2 fat
Grilled Chicken Sandwich	1 (6.25 oz.)	290	35	24	7	1	60	360	2 starch, 1 vegetable, 2 lean meat
Breaded Chicken Sandwich	1 (7.3 oz.)	450	44	26	20	4	60	740	3 starch, 2 med. fat meat, 2 fat
Chicken Club Sandwich	1 (7.75 oz.)	520	44	30	25	6	75	980	3 starch, 3 med. fat meat, 2 fat
Jr. Hamburger	(4 oz.)	270	34	15	9	3	35	590	2 starch, 1½ med. fat meat
Jr. Cheeseburger	1 (4.5 oz.)	320	34	18	13	5	45	760	2 starch, 2 med. fat meat
🅱 Jr. Bacon Cheeseburger	1 (6 oz.)	440	33	22	25	8	65	330	2 starch, 2 med. fat meat, 3 fat
Jr. Cheeseburger Deluxe	1 (6.3 oz.)	390	36	18	20	7	50	320	2 starch, 2 vegetable, 2 med. fat meat, 2 fat
Hamburger, Kids' Meal	1 (4 oz.)	270	33	15	9	3	35	210	2 starch, 1½ med. fat meat
Cheeseburger, Kids' Meal	1 (4.3 oz.)	310	33	18	13	5	45	760	2 starch, 2 med. fat meat
Sandwich Components ¼ lb. Hamburger Patty	1 (2.6 oz.)	190	tr	19	12	5	70	220	3 med. fat meat
American Cheese Slice	1 slice	70	tr	4	6	4	15	260	1 med. fat meat
Bacon	1 strip	30	tr	2	2	1	5	125	1 fat
Ketchup	1 tsp.	7	2	tr	tr	tr	0	75	Free
Lettuce	1 leaf	2	tr	tr	tr	tr	0	tr	Free
Mayonnaise	2 tsp.	93	tr	tr	10	1	8	60	2 fats
Mustard	½ tsp.	4	tr	tr	tr	tr	0	65	Free
Onion	4 rings	2	tr	tr	tr	tr	0	tr	Free

🅱 = More than 2 fat exchanges per serving   🌡 = More than 800 milligrams sodium   🍬 = High amounts of sugar

Products	SERVING SIZE	CALORIES	CARBO-HYDRATE (gm)	PROTEIN (gm)	FAT (gm)	SAT. FAT (gm)	CHOLES-TEROL (mg)	SODIUM (mg)	Exchanges
Dill Pickles	4 slices	2	tr	tr	tr	tr	0	160	Free
Tomatoes	1 slice	6	1	tr	tr	tr	0	tr	Free
Red. Cal. Honey Mustard	1 tsp.	25	2	tr	2	tr	0	45	Free
☒ Tartar Sauce	1 Tbsp.	130	tr	tr	14	2	15	115	3 fat

Baked Potato

Products	SERVING SIZE	CALORIES	CARBO-HYDRATE (gm)	PROTEIN (gm)	FAT (gm)	SAT. FAT (gm)	CHOLES-TEROL (mg)	SODIUM (mg)	Exchanges
Plain	1 (10 oz.)	300	69	6	tr	tr	0	20	4 starch
☀ Bacon & Cheese	1 (13.4 oz.)	510	75	17	17	4	15	1170	5 starch, 1 med. fat meat, 2 fat
Broccoli & Cheese	1 (14.5 oz.)	450	77	9	14	2	0	450	5 starch, 2 fat
☒ Cheese	1 (13.5 oz.)	550	74	14	24	8	30	640	5 starch, 1 med. fat meat, 3 fat
Chili & Cheese	1 (15.5 oz.)	600	80	21	25	9	45	740	5 starch, 2 med. fat meat, 2 fat
Sour Cream & Chives	1 (11 oz.)	370	71	8	6	4	15	35	4½ starch, 1 fat
Sour Cream	1 pkt.	60	1	1	6	4	15	15	1 fat

French Fries, Nuggets, and Chili

Products	SERVING SIZE	CALORIES	CARBO-HYDRATE (gm)	PROTEIN (gm)	FAT (gm)	SAT. FAT (gm)	CHOLES-TEROL (mg)	SODIUM (mg)	Exchanges
Small	3.2 oz.	240	33	3	12	2	0	150	2 starch, 2 fat
☒ Medium	4.8 oz.	360	50	5	17	4	0	220	3 starch, 3 fat
☒ Biggie	6 oz.	450	62	6	22	5	0	280	4 starch, 4 fat
Chicken Nuggets	6 pieces	280	12	14	20	5	50	600	1 starch, 2 med. fat meat, 1 fat
Barbecue Sauce	1 pkt.	50	11	1	0	0	0	100	1 starch or fruit
Sweet & Sour Sauce	1 pkt.	45	11	1	tr	0	0	55	1 fruit
Sweet Mustard	1 pkt.	50	9	1	1	tr	0	140	1 fruit
Chili	Small (8 oz.)	190	21	19	6	2	40	670	1½ starch, 2 lean meat
☀ Chili	Large (12 oz.)	290	31	28	9	4	60	1000	2 starch, 3 lean meat
Cheddar Cheese,	2 Tbsp. shredded	70	1	4	6	4	20	120	1 med. fat meat

Products	SERVING SIZE	CALORIES	CARBO-HYDRATE (gm)	PROTEIN (gm)	FAT (gm)	SAT. FAT (gm)	CHOLES-TEROL (mg)	SODIUM (mg)	Exchanges
Saltine Crackers	6	75	12	2	3	tr	0	240	1 starch

Salads

Products	SERVING SIZE	CALORIES	CARBO-HYDRATE (gm)	PROTEIN (gm)	FAT (gm)	SAT. FAT (gm)	CHOLES-TEROL (mg)	SODIUM (mg)	Exchanges
Caesar Side Salad	1 (4.5 oz.)	160	18	10	6	1	10	700	3 vegetable or 1 starch, ½ med. fat meat, 1 fat
Deluxe Garden Salad	1 (9.6 oz.)	110	9	7	5	1	0	380	2 vegetable, 1 fat
Taco Salad	1 (18 oz.)	640	70	34	30	12	80	960	2 vegetable, 4 starch, 3 med. fat meat, 2 fat
Taco Sauce	1 pkg.	10	tr	tr	tr	0	0	105	Free
Grilled Chicken Salad	1 (12 oz.)	200	9	25	8	1	55	690	2 vegetable, 3 lean meat
Side Salad	1 (6.6 oz.)	60	4	3	tr	0	0	200	1 vegetable, 1 fat
Breadstick	1 (1.5 oz.)	130	24	4	3	1	5	250	1½ starch

Garden Spot Salad Bar

Products	SERVING SIZE	CALORIES	CARBO-HYDRATE (gm)	PROTEIN (gm)	FAT (gm)	SAT. FAT (gm)	CHOLES-TEROL (mg)	SODIUM (mg)	Exchanges
Lettuce, Iceberg or Romaine	3 cup	29	6	2	tr	tr	0	20	1 vegetable
	1 cup	10	2	1	tr	tr	0	5	Free
Alfalfa Sprouts	½ cup	4	1	1	tr	tr	0	tr	Free
Applesauce	2 Tbsp.	30	8	tr	tr	tr	0	tr	½ fruit
Bacon Bits	2 Tbsp.	45	1	5	2	1	5	430	½ med. fat meat
Bread Sticks	4	56	8	1	1	tr	0	100	½ starch
Broccoli	¼ cup	4	1	tr	tr	tr	0	tr	Free
Cantaloupe, sliced	1 piece	16	4	tr	tr	tr	0	tr	Free
Carrots	¼ cup	6	2	tr	tr	tr	0	5	Free
Cauliflower	¼ cup	4	1	tr	tr	tr	0	tr	Free
Cheddar Chips	2 Tbsp.	70	5	1	5	1	0	170	1 fat
Cheese, shredded	2 Tbsp.	50	1	4	4	1	0	280	½ med. fat meat
Chicken Salad	2 Tbsp.	70	2	4	5	1	0	135	1 med. fat meat
Chow Mein Noodles	¼ cup	35	4	1	2	tr	0	55	Free
California Cole Slaw	2 Tbsp.	45	5	tr	3	tr	5	60	1 vegetable, 1 fat
Cottage Cheese	1 Tbsp.	30	1	4	1	1	5	125	½ lean meat

8 = More than 2 fat exchanges per serving   🖈 = More than 800 milligrams sodium   🍬 = High amounts of sugar

Products	SERVING SIZE	CALORIES	CARBO-HYDRATE (gm)	PROTEIN (gm)	FAT (gm)	SAT. FAT (gm)	CHOLES-TEROL (mg)	SODIUM (mg)	Exchanges
Croutons	¼ cup	30	8	2	2	tr	NA	130	½ starch
Cucumbers	2 slices	2	tr	tr	tr	tr	0	tr	Free
Eggs, hard cooked	2 Tbsp.	40	tr	3	3	1	120	30	½ med. fat meat
Garbanzo Beans	2 Tbsp.	45	7	2	1	tr	0	tr	½ starch
Green Peas	2 Tbsp.	20	3	1	tr	tr	0	25	Free
Green Pepper	2 pieces	2	1	tr	tr	tr	0	tr	Free
Honeydew Melon, sliced	1 piece	18	5	tr	tr	tr	0	5	Free
Jalapeno Peppers	1 Tbsp.	2	1	tr	tr	tr	0	160	Free
Mushrooms	¼ cup	14	1	tr	tr	tr	0	tr	Free
Olives, black	2 Tbsp.	16	1	tr	1	tr	0	120	Free
Orange, sectioned	1 piece	14	4	tr	tr	tr	0	0	Free
Pasta Salad	2 Tbsp.	80	11	2	4	NA	5	115	½ starch, 1 fat
Peaches, sliced	1 piece	20	6	tr	tr	tr	0	tr	Free
Pepperoni, sliced	6 pieces	30	tr	1	3	1	5	95	½ fat
Pineapple, chunked	4 piece	20	5	tr	tr	tr	0	tr	Free
Potato Salad	2 Tbsp.	70	4	tr	5	NA	NA	170	1 vegetable, 1 fat
♥ Pudding, Chocolate or Vanilla	¼ cup	80	10	1	3	NA	0	60	1 starch
Red Onions	3 rings	4	1	tr	tr	tr	0	tr	Free
Seafood Salad	¼ cup	70	5	3	4	1	0	300	½ med. fat meat
Strawberries	1 each	8	2	tr	tr	tr	0	tr	Free
♥ Strawberry Banana Dessert	¼ cup	110	28	1	tr	tr	0	tr	2 fruit
Sunflower Seeds & Raisins	2 Tbsp.	80	4	3	6	NA	0	tr	½ fruit, 1 fat
Three Bean Salad	2 Tbsp.	30	6	1	tr	tr	NA	10	1 vegetable
Tomato, wedged	1 piece	6	1	tr	tr	tr	0	tr	Free
Tuna Salad	2 Tbsp.	100	4	7	6	1	0	270	1 med. fat meat
Turkey Ham, diced	2 Tbsp.	30	1	4	12	tr	15	210	½ lean meat
Watermelon, wedged	1 piece	20	4	tr	tr	tr	0	tr	½ fruit

Products	SERVING SIZE	CALORIES	CARBO-HYDRATE (gm)	PROTEIN (gm)	FAT (gm)	SAT. FAT (gm)	CHOLES-TEROL (mg)	SODIUM (mg)	Exchanges
Salad Dressings (1 ladle equals 2 tablespoons)									
∄ Bleu Cheese	2 Tbsp.	180	tr	1	19	4	20	200	3 fat
Celery Seed	2 Tbsp.	130	6	tr	11	2	5	120	2 fat
French	2 Tbsp.	120	6	tr	10	2	0	330	2 fat
French, Sweet Red	2 Tbsp.	130	9	tr	10	2	0	230	2 fat
Hidden Valley Ranch	2 Tbsp.	100	1	1	10	2	10	220	2 fat
∄ Italian Caesar	2 Tbsp.	150	1	1	16	3	10	260	3 fat
Italian, Golden	2 Tbsp.	90	6	tr	7	1	0	460	1½ fat
Red. Cal. Bacon & Tomato	2 Tbsp.	90	5	tr	7	1	0	350	1½ fat
Red. Cal. Italian	2 Tbsp.	50	3	tr	4	1	0	340	1 fat
∄ Salad Oil	1 Tbsp.	120	0	0	14	2	0	0	3 fat
∄ Thousand Island	2 Tbsp.	130	3	tr	13	2	15	200	3 fat
Wine Vinegar	1 Tbsp.	2	tr	tr	tr	tr	0	tr	Free
Mexican Fiesta									
Cheese Sauce	¼ cup	40	5	1	2	tr	0	310	½ fat
Picante Sauce	2 Tbsp.	10	2	tr	tr	tr	NA	tr	Free
Refried Beans	¼ cup	70	9	3	2	1	0	200	1 starch
Spanish Rice	¼ cup	60	11	1	1	tr	NA	390	1 starch
Sour Topping	2 Tbsp.	45	1	1	4	NA	0	25	1 fat
Taco Chips	8 each	160	25	3	6	1	NA	15	1½ starch, 1 fat
Taco Meat	2 Tbsp.	80	2	7	4	1	15	200	1 med. fat meat
Taco Sauce	2 Tbsp.	12	2	tr	tr	tr	NA	110	Free
Taco Shells	2 each	100	12	2	6	NA	NA	90	1 starch, 1 fat
Tortilla, Flour	1 each	100	18	3	3	NA	NA	210	1 starch, 1 fat
Pasta Salad Bar									
Alfredo Sauce	¼ cup	30	4	1	1	tr	0	260	1 vegetable
Fettucini	½ cup	66	18	5	4	1	10	tr	1 starch
Garlic Toast	2 piece	140	18	4	6	2	0	40	1 starch, 1 fat
Macaroni & Cheese	½ cup	130	14	4	6	3	5	320	1 starch, 1 fat

∄ = More than 2 fat exchanges per serving   ∄ = More than 800 milligrams sodium   ♣ = High amounts of sugar

Products	SERVING SIZE	CALORIES	CARBO-HYDRATE (gm)	PROTEIN (gm)	FAT (gm)	SAT. FAT (gm)	CHOLES-TEROL (mg)	SODIUM (mg)	Exchanges
Pasta Medley	½ cup	60	8	2	2	tr	NA	tr	½ starch
Red Peppers, crushed	1 Tbsp.	20	3	1	1	tr	0	tr	Free
Roma/Parm Blend, grated	2 Tbsp.	70	5	3	3	2	10	250	1 med. fat meat
Rotini	½ cup	90	15	3	2	tr	NA	NA	1 starch
Spaghetti Sauce	¼ cup	30	6	1	tr	tr	0	340	1 vegetable
Spaghetti Meat Sauce	¼ cup	45	6	3	1	1	5	230	1 vegetable

OCCASIONAL USE

Products	SERVING SIZE	CALORIES	CARBO-HYDRATE (gm)	PROTEIN (gm)	FAT (gm)	SAT. FAT (gm)	CHOLES-TEROL (mg)	SODIUM (mg)	Exchanges
♥ Frosty Dairy Dessert	Small (12 oz.)	340	57	9	10	5	40	200	4 starch, 2 fat
♥ Chocolate Chip Cookie	1 each	280	39	3	13	4	15	260	2½ starch, 2 fat

NOT RECOMMENDED FOR USE

Products	SERVING SIZE	CALORIES	CARBO-HYDRATE (gm)	PROTEIN (gm)	FAT (gm)	SAT. FAT (gm)	CHOLES-TEROL (mg)	SODIUM (mg)	Exchanges
♥ Frosty Dairy Dessert	Medium (16 oz.)	460	76	12	13	7	55	260	
♥ Frosty Dairy Dessert	Large (20 oz.)	570	95	15	17	9	70	330	

WHATABURGER

Sandwiches

Products	SERVING SIZE	CALORIES	CARBO-HYDRATE (gm)	PROTEIN (gm)	FAT (gm)	SAT. FAT (gm)	CHOLES-TEROL (mg)	SODIUM (mg)	Exchanges
♟ Whataburger	1 (10.6 oz.)	580	58	32	24	NA	70	1092	4 starch, 3 med. fat meat, 2 fat
☗♟ Whataburger w/Cheese	1 (11.5 oz.)	669	58	36	33	NA	96	1474	4 starch, 3½ med. fat meat, 3 fat
Whataburger Jr.	1 (5.4 oz.)	304	31	15	14	NA	30	684	2 starch, 1 med. fat meat, 2 fat
☗♟ Whataburger Jr. w/Cheese	1 (5.8 oz.)	351	30	17	18	NA	42	921	2 starch, 1 med. fat meat, 3 fat
Justaburger	1 (4 oz.)	265	28	12	12	NA	25	547	2 starch, 1 med. fat meat, 1 fat
Justaburger w/Cheese	1 (4.5 oz.)	312	28	15	16	NA	37	784	2 starch, 1 med. fat meat, 2 fat
☗ Whatacatch	1 (6.2 oz.)	475	43	14	27	NA	34	722	3 starch, 1 med. fat meat, 4 fat

Products	SERVING SIZE	CALORIES	CARBO-HYDRATE (gm)	PROTEIN (gm)	FAT (gm)	SAT. FAT (gm)	CHOLES-TEROL (mg)	SODIUM (mg)	Exchanges
🅱 🌡 Whatacatch w/Cheese	1 (6.7 oz.)	522	43	16	32	NA	45	959	3 starch, 1 med. fat meat, 5 fat
🌡 Whataburger Double Meat	1 (13.5 oz.)	806	59	51	41	NA	154	1296	4 starch, 5 med. fat meat, 2 fat
🅱 🌡 Whataburger Double Meat w/Cheese	1 (14.4 oz.)	895	59	55	49	NA	180	1678	4 starch, 6½ med. fat meat, 3 fat
🅱 🌡 Whatachicken Sandwich	1 (10 oz.)	671	61	35	32	NA	71	1460	4 starch, 3 med. fat meat, 3 fat
Ground Beef Patty	¼ lb.	226	1	19	17	NA	84	232	3 med. fat meat
Ground Beef Patty	⅒ lb.	90	tr	8	6	NA	34	81	1 high fat meat
Bun	5 inch	290	56	10	3	NA	tr	532	4 starch
Bun	4 inch	150	29	5	2	NA	tr	274	2 starch
🌡 Fajita Taco	1 (6 oz.)	301	27	23	11	NA	55	1070	2 starch, 2 med. fat meat

Side Orders

Products	SERVING SIZE	CALORIES	CARBO-HYDRATE (gm)	PROTEIN (gm)	FAT (gm)	SAT. FAT (gm)	CHOLES-TEROL (mg)	SODIUM (mg)	Exchanges
French Fries	Small	221	25	4	12	NA	tr	50	1½ starch, 1 fat
🅱 French Fries	Regular	332	37	5	18	NA	tr	45	2½ starch, 3 fat
🅱 Onions Rings	1 order	226	22	4	13	NA	tr	410	1½ starch, 3 fat
Taquito	1 (4.4 oz.)	310	17	19	19	NA	223	712	1 starch, 2 med. fat meat, 2 fat
🌡 Taquito w/Cheese	1 (4.8 oz.)	357	17	21	23	NA	235	949	1 starch, 3 med. fat meat, 1 fat
🌡 Taquito Ranchero	1 (5.4 oz.)	320	19	19	18	NA	223	1092	1 starch, 2 med. fat meat, 2 fat
🅱 🌡 Taquito Ranchero w/Cheese	1 (5.8 oz.)	367	19	21	23	NA	235	1329	1 starch, 2 med. fat meat, 3 fat

Breakfast Items

Products	SERVING SIZE	CALORIES	CARBO-HYDRATE (gm)	PROTEIN (gm)	FAT (gm)	SAT. FAT (gm)	CHOLES-TEROL (mg)	SODIUM (mg)	Exchanges
Egg Omelette Sandwich	1 (4.2 oz.)	312	29	14	15	NA	191	696	2 starch, 1 med. fat meat, 2 fat
🌡 Egg Omelette Sandwich Ranchero	1 (5.2 oz.)	322	31	15	16	NA	191	1067	2 starch, 1 med. fat meat, 2 fat

🅱 = More than 2 fat exchanges per serving   🌡 = More than 800 milligrams sodium   ♠ = High amounts of sugar

Products	SERVING SIZE	CALORIES	CARBO-HYDRATE (gm)	PROTEIN (gm)	FAT (gm)	SAT. FAT (gm)	CHOLES-TEROL (mg)	SODIUM (mg)	Exchanges
Pancakes w/out Syrup & Butter	1 order	288	54	9	4	NA	49	977	3½ starch, 1 fat
Sausage	1 order	208	1	9	19	NA	43	355	1 high fat meat, 2 fat
Breakfast on ½ Bun	1 (6.2 oz.)	520	29	23	34	NA	234	1051	2 starch, 2 med. fat meat, 5 fat
Breakfast on ½ Bun Ranchero	1 (7.2 oz.)	530	32	23	35	NA	236	1431	2 starch, 2 med. fat meat, 5 fat

OCCASIONAL USE

Products	SERVING SIZE	CALORIES	CARBO-HYDRATE (gm)	PROTEIN (gm)	FAT (gm)	SAT. FAT (gm)	CHOLES-TEROL (mg)	SODIUM (mg)	Exchanges
Apple Pie	1	236	30	3	12	NA	tr	265	2 starch, 2 fat
Pecan Danish	1	270	28	5	16	NA	12	419	2 starch, 3 fat
Vanilla Shake	Small	322	50	9	9	NA	37	169	3 starch, 2 fat

NOT RECOMMENDED FOR USE

Products	SERVING SIZE	CALORIES	CARBO-HYDRATE (gm)	PROTEIN (gm)	FAT (gm)	SAT. FAT (gm)	CHOLES-TEROL (mg)	SODIUM (mg)	Exchanges
Vanilla Shake	Medium	439	68	12	13	NA	51	230	
Vanilla Shake	Large	657	102	19	19	NA	75	874	
Vanilla Shake	Extra Large	877	137	25	26	NA	100	1168	

WHITE CASTLE

Sandwiches

Products	SERVING SIZE	CALORIES	CARBO-HYDRATE (gm)	PROTEIN (gm)	FAT (gm)	SAT. FAT (gm)	CHOLES-TEROL (mg)	SODIUM (mg)	Exchanges
Hamburger	1 (2 oz.)	161	15	6	8	NA	NA	266	1 starch, 1 high fat meat
Cheeseburger	1 (2.3 oz.)	200	15	8	11	NA	NA	361	1 starch, 1 high fat meat, 1 fat
Fish w/out Tartar Sauce	1 (2.1 oz.)	155	21	6	5	NA	NA	201	1½ starch, ½ high fat meat
Sausage & Egg Sandwich	1 order	322	16	13	22	NA	NA	698	1 starch, 2 med. fat meat, 2 fat
Sausage Sandwich	1 (1.7 oz.)	196	13	7	12	NA	NA	488	1 starch, 1 med. fat meat, 1 fat
Chicken Sandwich	1 (2.3 oz.)	186	21	8	7	NA	NA	497	1½ starch, 1 med. fat meat

Products	SERVING SIZE	CALORIES	CARBO-HYDRATE (gm)	PROTEIN (gm)	FAT (gm)	SAT. FAT (gm)	CHOLES-TEROL (mg)	SODIUM (mg)	Exchanges
Side Orders									
ⓑ French Fries	1 order (3.4 oz.)	301	38	2	15	NA	NA	193	2½ starch, 3 fat
Onion Rings	1 order (2.1 oz.)	245	27	3	13	NA	NA	566	2 starch, 2 fat
ⓑ ⓣ Onion Chips	1 order (3.3 oz.)	329	39	4	17	NA	NA	832	2½ starch, 3 fat

ⓑ = More than 2 fat exchanges per serving   ⓣ = More than 800 milligrams sodium   ⓦ = High amounts of sugar

Products	SERVING SIZE	CALORIES	CARBO-HYDRATE (gm)	PROTEIN (gm)	FAT (gm)	SAT. FAT (gm)	CHOLES-TEROL (mg)	SODIUM (mg)	Exchanges

IN CANADA

To convert American exchanges to Canadian exchanges, see chart on page 112.

HARVEY'S FOODS

Products	SERVING SIZE	CALORIES	CARBO-HYDRATE (gm)	PROTEIN (gm)	FAT (gm)	SAT. FAT (gm)	CHOLES-TEROL (mg)	SODIUM (mg)	Exchanges
Hamburger	1	357	32	18	18	7	45	1000	2 starch, 2 med. fat meat, 1 fat
Cheeseburger	1	418	33	22	22	10	51	1087	2 starch, 2½ med. fat meat, 2 fat
Double Burger	1	609	32	33	39	14	83	1540	2 starch, 4 med. fat meat, 3 fat
Super Burger	1	518	40	24	29	10	72	790	2½ starch, 3 med. fat meat, 2 fat
Junior Burger	1	236	25	13	10	4	22	410	1½ starch, 1½ med. fat meat
Light Burger	1	311	34	18	11	4	37	1000	2 starch, 2 med. fat meat
Hot Dog	1	313	39	13	12	4	43	220	2½ starch, 1 med. fat meat, 1 fat
Fish Sandwich	1	393	49	15	15	2	17	750	3 starch, 1 med. fat meat, 2 fat
Chicken Sandwich	1	375	38	20	16	3	36	1072	2½ starch, 2 med. fat meat, 1 fat
Charbroiled Chicken Sandwich	1	264	36	19	5	1	37	285	2 starch, 2 lean meat
Chicken Fingers	5	234	15	17	12	1	30	540	1 starch, 2 med. fat meat
Condiments									
Plum Sauce	1.5 oz.	69	17	0	0	0	0	345	1 fruit
Sweet & Sour Sauce	1.5 oz.	49	13	tr	0	0	0	63	1 fruit
Honey Mustard Sauce	1.5 oz.	78	20	tr	tr	0	0	160	1 fruit
Barbeque Sauce	1.5 oz.	56	14	1	tr	0	0	380	1 starch
Side Orders									
French Fries	Regular	385	54	5	16	2	2	250	3½ starch, 2 fat

Products	SERVING SIZE	CALORIES	CARBO-HYDRATE (gm)	PROTEIN (gm)	FAT (gm)	SAT. FAT (gm)	CHOLES-TEROL (mg)	SODIUM (mg)	Exchanges
🛢 French Fries	Large	526	74	7	22	3	2	340	5 starch, 3 fat
🛢 Onion Rings	1 order	286	23	4	20	2	tr	580	1½ starch, 4 fat
🛢 Poutine	1 order	738	69	19	43	11	15	275	4½ starch, 1 med. fat meat, 7 fat
Gravy	1 order	35	5	1	1	tr	tr	200	Free
🌡 Vegetable Soup	1 order	80	17	1	1	tr	tr	1094	1 starch
Salad	1 serving	103	6	1	7	tr	106	137	1 vegetable, 1 fat

Salad Dressings

Products	SERVING SIZE	CALORIES	CARBO-HYDRATE (gm)	PROTEIN (gm)	FAT (gm)	SAT. FAT (gm)	CHOLES-TEROL (mg)	SODIUM (mg)	Exchanges
Fat Free Italian	1.5 oz.	14	3	tr	0	0	0	462	Free
Light French	1.5 oz.	68	8	tr	4	tr	tr	457	1 fat
🛢 Ranch	1.5 oz.	205	3	1	21	2	8	343	4 fat
🛢 Feta	1.5 oz.	170	2	1	17	2	14	396	3 fat

Breakfast Items

Products	SERVING SIZE	CALORIES	CARBO-HYDRATE (gm)	PROTEIN (gm)	FAT (gm)	SAT. FAT (gm)	CHOLES-TEROL (mg)	SODIUM (mg)	Exchanges
Western Sandwich	1	370	52	8	15	6	134	731	3 starch, 1 med. fat meat, 2 fat
Eggs Fried	2	174	2	13	13	3	290	140	2 med. fat meat, 1 fat
Bacon	3 slices	103	0	8	8	3	16	320	1 high fat meat
Breakfast Sausage	1 order	137	3	8	11	5	31	270	1 med. fat meat, 1 fat
🌡 Home Fries	1 order	272	38	5	11	2	tr	923	2½ starch, 2 fat
Toast Buttered	1 order	306	38	9	13	7	20	490	2½ starch, 2 fat
🍯 Strawberry Jam	1 order	50	13	0	0	0	0	5	1 fruit
🍯 Orange Marmalade	1 order	56	14	tr	0	0	0	9	1 fruit
🍯 Honey	1 order	64	17	tr	0	0	0	1	1 fruit
Peanut Butter	1 order	115	3	4	10	2	1	86	1 high fat meat
🛢🌡 Bacon, Egg, Tomato Sandwich	1	500	40	23	28	11	180	882	2 starch, 2 vegetable, 2 med. fat meat, 3 fat
🛢🌡 Sausage, Egg, Tomato	1	534	43	23	30	13	196	832	2 starch, 2 vegetable, 2 med. fat meat, 4 fat
🌡 Pancakes	2	223	42	7	3	1	10	870	3 starch
🍯 Pancake Syrup	1 order	166	42	0	0	0	0	1	3 fruit

🛢 = More than 2 fat exchanges per serving   🌡 = More than 800 milligrams sodium   🍯 = High amounts of sugar

Products	SERVING SIZE	CALORIES	CARBO-HYDRATE (gm)	PROTEIN (gm)	FAT (gm)	SAT. FAT (gm)	CHOLES-TEROL (mg)	SODIUM (mg)	Exchanges
🛢 Muffin Bran	1	401	53	6	16	tr	tr	350	3½ starch, 3 fat
Muffin Blueberry	1	320	57	5	8	tr	tr	273	3 starch, ½ fruit, 1 fat
Orange Juice	1 order	78	18	1	tr	tr	0	4	1 fruit
Apple Juice	1 order	87	19	1	tr	tr	0	5	1 fruit

OCCASIONAL USE

Products	SERVING SIZE	CALORIES	CARBO-HYDRATE (gm)	PROTEIN (gm)	FAT (gm)	SAT. FAT (gm)	CHOLES-TEROL (mg)	SODIUM (mg)	Exchanges
🛢 Apple Turnover	1	243	25	3	15	4	2	310	1½ starch, 3 fat
🍷 Chocolate Milkshake	1	364	59	11	9	5	27	190	4 starch, 1 fat
🍷 Vanilla Milkshake	1	370	59	11	10	5	28	120	4 starch, 1 fat
🍷 Strawberry Milkshake	1	356	56	12	9	5	25	130	4 starch, 1 fat
🛢 Ice Burger	1	374	37	3	25	tr	tr	139	2½ starch, 4 fat

SWISS CHALET

Entrees

Products	SERVING SIZE	CALORIES	CARBO-HYDRATE (gm)	PROTEIN (gm)	FAT (gm)	SAT. FAT (gm)	CHOLES-TEROL (mg)	SODIUM (mg)	Exchanges
Chicken White (with skin)	Quarter	381	0	47	22	4	159	175	7 lean meat
Chicken White (skinless)	Quarter	225	0	40	8	2	114	84	5½ lean meat
Chicken Dark (with skin)	Quarter	313	0	40	17	5	175	200	5½ lean meat
Chicken Dark (skinless)	Quarter	232	0	35	10	3	160	130	5 lean meat
Chicken	Half (with skin)	694	0	87	39	9	334	375	12 lean meat
⚕ BBQ Chicken Sandwich & Sauce	1	744	54	54	20	5	143	924	4 starch, 6 lean meat
Back Rib	Half	405	6	37	26	9	115	304	5 med. fat meat
Back Rib	Full	810	12	74	52	18	230	608	1 starch, 10 med. fat meat
🛢⚕ Chicken Pot Pie	1	494	53	17	24	5	64	951	3 starch, 1 vegetable, 1 med. fat meat, 4 fat

Products	SERVING SIZE	CALORIES	CARBO-HYDRATE (gm)	PROTEIN (gm)	FAT (gm)	SAT. FAT (gm)	CHOLES-TEROL (mg)	SODIUM (mg)	Exchanges
Chicken Salad & Roll	1	466	34	31	22	4	206	493	2 starch, 4 med. fat meat

Side Orders

Products	SERVING SIZE	CALORIES	CARBO-HYDRATE (gm)	PROTEIN (gm)	FAT (gm)	SAT. FAT (gm)	CHOLES-TEROL (mg)	SODIUM (mg)	Exchanges
Roll	1	116	24	3	1	tr	1	514	1½ starch
Fries	1 order	442	53	8	22	5	3	180	3½ starch, 4 fat
Baked Potato	1	272	62	6	tr	tr	0	19	4 starch
Chalet Chicken Soup	1 order	97	11	9	2	tr	1	820	1 starch, 1 lean meat
Chalet Salad	1	33	7	3	0	0	0	26	1 vegetable
House Dressing	1 order	128	6	0	11	tr	1	386	2 fat
Low-Cal Italian Dressing	1 order	1	0	1	tr	tr	tr	395	Free
Caesar Salad	Entree	690	24	4	38	4	20	800	1 starch, 1 vegetable, 8 fat
Caesar Salad	Appetizer	345	12	2	19	2	10	400	1 starch, 4 fat

OCCASIONAL USE

Products	SERVING SIZE	CALORIES	CARBO-HYDRATE (gm)	PROTEIN (gm)	FAT (gm)	SAT. FAT (gm)	CHOLES-TEROL (mg)	SODIUM (mg)	Exchanges
Apple Pie	1	413	59	3	19	4	1	328	2 starch, 2 fruit 3 fat
Ice Cream	1 order	195	16	3	14	6	50	65	1 starch, 3 fat
Yogurt	1 order	178	28	5	5	3	15	96	2 starch

B = More than 2 fat exchanges per serving   ▲ = More than 800 milligrams sodium   ♥ = High amounts of sugar

Comparison of American and Canadian Food Group Systems

American Diabetes Association Exchange System		Canadian Diabetes Association Choice System
1 Starch	=	1 Starchy Foods
1 Lean Meat	=	1 Protein Foods
1 Medium-Fat Meat	=	1 Protein + 1/2 Fats & Oils
1 High-Fat Meat	=	1 Protein + 1 Fats & Oils
1 Vegetable	=	1/2 Fruits & Vegetables
(no equivalent)	=	Extra Vegetables
1 Fruit	=	1 1/2 Fruits & Vegetables
1 Milk	=	2 Milk (Skim)
1 Fat	=	1 Fats & Oils

Canadian Diabetes Association.
Comparison of American and Canadian food group systems.
Diabetes Dialogue, 1988; 35 (4):57.

CHRONIMED PUBLISHING
BOOKS OF RELATED INTEREST

Fast Food Facts by Marion Franz, M.S., R.D., C.D.E. This revised and up-to-date best-seller shows how to make smart nutrition choices at fast food restaurants—and tells what to avoid. Includes complete nutrition information on more than 1,500 menu offerings from the 37 largest fast food chains.
Standard-size edition (7 1/2" x 8 1/2")

004240	ISBN 1-56561-043-1	$7.95

Pocket edition (4" x 5 1/2")

004228	ISBN 1-56561-031-8	$4.95

Convenience Food Facts by Arlene Monk, R.D., C.D.E., with introduction by Marion Franz, M.S., R.D., C.D.E. Includes complete nutrition information, tips, and exchange values on more than 1,500 popular brand-name processed foods commonly found in grocery store freezers and shelves. Helps you plan easy-to-prepare, nutritious meals.

004081	ISBN 0-937721-77-8	$10.95

Exchanges for All Occasions by Marion Franz, M.S., R.D., C.D.E. Here's a book that helps everyone to effectively use the popular exchange system for meal planning. This updated and revised edition includes planning suggestions for just about any occasion, sample meal plans, special instructions for people with diabetes, and more.

004201	ISBN 1-56561-005-9	$12.95

The Joy of Snacks by Nancy Cooper, R.D. Offers more than 200 delicious recipes and nutrition information for hearty snacks, including sandwiches, appetizers, soups, spreads, cookies, muffins, and treats especially for kids. The book also suggests guidelines for selecting convenience snacks and interpreting information on food labels.

004086	ISBN 0-937721-82-4	$12.95

The Healthy Eater's Guide to Family & Chain Restaurants by Hope S. Warshaw, M.M.Sc., R.D. Here's the only guide that tells you how to eat healthier in over 100 of America's most popular family and chain restaurants. It offers complete and up-to-date nutrition information and suggests which items to choose and avoid.

004214	ISBN 1-56561-017-2	$9.95

Fight Fat & Win by Elaine Moquette-Magee, M.P.H., R.D. This breakthrough book explains how to easily lower the fat in everything you eat, from fast food and common restaurants to quick meals at home, simply by making smarter choices.

004244	ISBN 1-56561-047-4	$9.95

How Should I Feed My Child? From Pregnancy to Preschool by Sandra Nissenberg, M.S., R.D., Margaret Bogle, Ph.D., R.D., Edna Langholz, M.S., R.D., and Audrey Wright, M.S., R.D. Addressing real issues and parents' most common concerns, this guide tells how to start your child off to a lifetime of good eating habits. Includes over 50 recipes.
"From four nutrition experts with impressive credentials, the book offers easy-to-read, practical advice."
-USA *Today*
* A Doubleday Health Book Club Selection
        004232   ISBN 1-56561-035-0 $12.95

200 Kid-Tested Ways to Lower the Fat in Your Child's Favorite Foods by Elaine Moquette-Magee, M.P.H., R.D. For the first time ever, here's a much needed and asked for guide that gives easy, step-by-step instructions on cutting the fat in the most popular brand name and homemade foods kids eat every day—without them even noticing.
* A Doubleday Health Book Club Selection
        004231   ISBN 1-56561-034-2 $12.95

All-American Low-Fat Meals in Minutes by M.J. Smith, M.A., R.D., L.D. Filled with tantalizing recipes and valuable tips, this cookbook makes great-tasting, low-fat foods a snap for holidays, special occasions, or everyday. Most recipes take only minutes to prepare.
        004079   ISBN 0-937721-73-5 $12.95

60 Days of Low-Fat, Low-Cost Meals in Minutes by M.J. Smith, R.D., L.D., M.A. Following the path of the best-seller *All American Low-Fat Meals in Minutes*, here are more than 150 quick and sumptuous recipes complete with the latest exchange values and nutrition facts for lowering calories, fat, salt, and cholesterol. This book contains complete menus for 60 days and recipes that use ingredients found in virtually any grocery store—most for a total cost of less than $10.
        004205   ISBN 1-56561-010-5 $12.95

The Guiltless Gourmet by Judy Gilliard and Joy Kirkpatrick, R.D. A perfect fusion of sound nutrition and creative cooking, this book is loaded with delicious recipes high in flavor and low in fat, sugar, calories, cholesterol, and salt.
        004021   ISBN 0-937721-23-9 $9.95

The Guiltless Gourmet Goes Ethnic by Judy Gilliard and Joy Kirkpatrick, R.D. More than a cookbook, this sequel to *The Guiltless Gourmet* shows how easy it is to lower the sugar, calories, sodium, and fat in your favorite ethnic dishes—without sacrificing taste.
        004072   ISBN 0-937721-68-9 $11.95

European Cuisine from the Guiltless Gourmet by Judy Gilliard and Joy Kirkpatrick, R.D. This book shows you how to lower the sugar, salt, cholesterol, total fat, and calories in delicious Greek, English, German, Russian, and Scandinavian dishes. Plus, it features complete nutrition information and the latest exchange values.
        004085   ISBN 0-937721-81-6 $11.95

Beyond Alfalfa Sprouts & Cheese: The Healthy Meatless Cookbook by Judy Gilliard and Joy Kirkpatrick, R.D., includes creative and savory meatless dishes using ingredients found in just about every grocery store. It also contains helpful cooking tips, complete nutrition information, and the latest exchange values.

004218   ISBN 1-56561-020-2 $12.95

One Year of Healthy, Hearty, & Simple One-Dish Meals by Pam Spaude and Jan Owan-McMenamin, R.D., is a collection of 365 easy-to-make healthy and tasty family favorites and unique creations that are meals in themselves. Most of the dishes take under 30 minutes to prepare.

004217   ISBN 1-56561-019-9 $12.95

Let Them Eat Cake by Virginia N. White with Rosa A. Mo, R.D. If you're looking for delicious and healthy pies, cookies, puddings, and cakes, this book will give you your just desserts. With easy, step-by-step instructions, this innovative cookbook features complete nutrition information, the latest exchange values, and tips on making your favorite snacks more healthful.

004206   ISBN 1-56561-011-3 $12.95

CHRONIMED Publishing
P.O. Box 47945
Minneapolis, MN 55447-9727

Circle the book (s) you would like sent. Enclosed is $_____.   (Please add $3.00 to this order to cover postage and handling. Minnesota residents add 6.5% sales tax.) Send check or money order, no cash or C.O.D.'s. Prices are subject to change without notice.

Name _____

Address _____

City _____ State _____ Zip _____

Allow 4 to 6 weeks for delivery.
Quantity discounts available upon request.

Or order by phone: 1-800-848-2793,
612-546-1146 (Minneapolis/St. Paul metro area).
Please have your credit card number ready.